Find Your Rainbow -
I Already Found Mine

Dominick A. Nisi

1

Find Your Rainbow- I Already Found Mine
By: Dominick A. Nisi

Introduction

Sept.19,2021

If you decide to read a piece twice, that's OK …. it's your book. If you decide to discard it that's not OK, pass it on, someone may find it of interest. I start with this Introduction; this book being made up of short stories may not be truly representative as a "BOOK". However, this is the closest I can come. A few of the narratives are informative to tell of my motivation, and the spirit and purpose of this book. Not to be redundant, I will let all that stand to serve itself. But this is a convenient place for me to embellish this promotion.

This was truly an uphill struggle for me. The words and thoughts came easy. It was everything else that was hard. The academic organizing required most of my efforts, and principally the typing. I ultimately ended up doing a good part of it myself, along, with a great deal of help. This became my "baptismal" into computers. All out of sheer necessity, enter my new laptop, courtesy of my Tutini family. Which I immediately named:" Becky." because she beckoned to me. Quite a historic struggle, still ongoing, but whatever?

Writing a book is a major challenge, however, very rewarding, particularly upon completion I weeded out some controversial subject matter to keep the book uncontroversial or neutral, intentionally omitting indifferent subject matter. Trying to stay or keep unbiased and not one-sided. I may be redundant with some themes, but that is the inevitable with interfacing matters such as family, love and so on.

This book is not intended as a commercial endeavor, However If I am fortunate enough to publish and sell a few copies, that's OK too.

Editorial note: Throughout my book, you might notice capitalizations that you would not normally see or expect. This is intended to show how important these are to me. A stylistic choice if you will. I may be grammatically or otherwise incorrect, but this is also to show the intent of my expressions.

Dedication

To My Beloved Wife For 65 Years and Our Children's' Mother…

Virginia Valle Nisi 1935-1975. Now In Heaven.

Prologue

Oct 16, 2021

As a prologue, this book started simply as one short Christmas story. Then prompted for a Sequel. Then on to additional thoughts all to be documented as narratives and now as my book. Made up of a variety of subjects all as thoughts casually occurring in my mind. An effort was made to organize the subjects into their similar categories to complete as a book to make for interesting reading.

Cover

The drawing depicted on the cover is the artistic rendering of Dominick A. Nisi, author.

ACKNOWLEDGEMENTS

I wish to thank all those that helped and encouraged me with my book. Starting with my immediate family: My adult children and their spouses: Diana, Marc, Anthony, Colleen, Karen, and Lou.

My Grandchildren And their spouses: Domenico, Krystal, Tiana, Edwin, Jiovanni, Emilee, Thalia, Isabela, Domenique, Antonio, Anthony and Harmony.

And now for our fourth generation: My Great Grandchildren: Grace and Estelle.

And many thanks to all others for their help and support: My Publisher, Linda Lucas, Friend and Journalist, Curtis J. Quinn and Friend and Guitar Instructor: Frank Rudolph. All without Whose Help Love and Friendship This Book Would Never Have Been Written.

My Flag

Narrative No.1
October 17th, 2020

I share it with all my fellow Americans I don't own it, but I served it, and served it with honor, today waving and unfurling in the sunshine, yesterday in the rain and so often in battle. I share My Flag with all Americans. All of us are so proud of what it stands for. The stars with blue background, the seven red stripes with six white ones. Each state is represented here, on our road map to liberty and freedom.

I cannot help but get teary eyed looking at my flag knowing all the sacrifices made for it as our country. What a gift to have this one symbol as a whole nation with all the country and all its people. It waves so proudly, how can words start to describe My Flag Just look and feel your heartbeat quicken with such a precious gift to have and to be a part of and to believe in what it represents.

I slept with my flag one night recently, just by chance, reminding me of when I slept with my rifle on the ground and in the snow on foreign soil. Ready and prepared to defend my Flag and my country a long, long time ago. I can only hope and pray that all Americans can appreciate what our Flag has always stood for in the past, in the present, and with God's help in the future. It waves right now to all Americans with the same message of love for their country and fellow man.

My Flag is a part of my life. I am privileged to know that have it, and to feel it. Also sharing my Flag with all others. Red, White, and Blue are so perfect along with the Shining Stars. May America's future be strong and survive all challenges and allow our country and our people to enjoy life with all liberties endowed by God and symbolized by My Flag.

Becky

Narrative No. 2
August 1, 2021

Three pieces typed so far with my newfound friend "Becky". That's her here right now, right this very moment, right with these very words. What a wonderful feeling, a feeling of exhilaration (wow a five-syllable word coming from me?) That's where Becky has brought me. Now to be capable of doing my own thing, my own typing, and not to have to depend on others. This freedom, this advantage is so enthralled in my mind because of the restraint the typing part of writing has been. Generally, my writing is unrestrained, my writing has been free flowing, just documenting whatever thoughts cross my mind mostly into the form of a narrative. Not to be vain and assume all my thoughts are interesting or would be interesting to all readers in book form. However, it fascinates me to read my own tales. Basically, all my different stories are simply my attempt to preserve a special moment though more for my immediate self, and not to lose it.

This really started with me during the Christmas season, 2019. A very mysterious sensation overcame me. This I believe is reflected in most of my stories, most with a message of some kind. My first narrative being "A Christmas Story" Narrative number 31. Only to be read and then perhaps to understand my motivation to write.

As closure, Becky now as my sweet laptop a Godsend allowing me to do my own typing and not having to depend on others. I now feel that my book will serve in part as my legacy to my family. Let it be known this laptop was gifted to me by my dearly beloved TUTINI family. I thank them wholeheartedly and then some.

My Fantasy

Having difficulty getting my stories typed. Down to one volunteer...My granddaughter, Tiana. However, the progress is bitterly slow. I'm presently at a point ready to give up on my plan to develop my short stories in the form of a book. Perhaps this book plan is somewhat of a fantasy. Not many may really be interested in what I have to say. Scattered, unusual story thoughts and possibly some dull subject matter. The question in my mind is, who would be interested? I'm on the brink of giving up. At the early thoughts it was all exciting me collecting my impressions and with sincere efforts endeavoring to document them.

My efforts were by way of jotting down little notes here and there. It became ridiculous scribbling on scraps of paper backs of envelopes whatever was handy at that moment. The moment being whenever a thought or impression or mood would strike. Most often I can complete such an effort to record, usually to my satisfaction with a favorable result. Not on paper plates but in a more organized fashion now using a notebook. All with great expectations of ultimately writing a book. A book of short stories. But first to get into a dedicated typing mode, very challenging.

Almost ready to give up. I am truly bewildered to try to understand my motivation for writing at all. The fact of the matter is I have never had the slightest interest in writing. Reading, yes. I read voraciously for quite a few years, until now, with the weariness of my eyes. However, this writing obsession is an obsession. What am I trying to prove? Who am I trying to impress? No one, but it does please me writing my stories. So strange, when I do read one of my stories, I enjoy each one, hardly believing It was me who wrote them. Very strange indeed. Most of them have a message. Like I'm preaching about something. I like them all.

I feel like each one of my stories are my favorites. Sometimes I do get teary eyed... My Flag, Momma. All are from my heart. When I get kind feedback, I feel that's what I was trying for. Trying to share a message of some kind. Who am I? Certainly not a writer. Just someone with sometimes deep thoughts. Why me? Why now? Where do these thoughts come from? I do realize that my wording is all very simple, far from eloquent. Not even that good. But it pleases me when I see what I was able to do.

Very impressive to me. Not at all as planned or programmed, just kind of natural. Natural in a sense of free flowing.

When I write and compose it's without much effort or premeditation, or planning. I think that's what pleases me the most. All free flowing. I like my own analogy. Like squeezing the toothpaste tube, and it just comes out. All free flowing. My subject matter is mixed and mostly unrelated. Unrelated to each other. I wonder what may provoke a thought at times. I sometimes am impressed with the continuity of the thought. Is that truly the way it should happen? All those thoughts, where do they come from? What brings them on. It is kind of a fun experience and certainly a challenge each time. I sometimes feel like I'm climbing Mt. Everest or swimming the English Channel. Look at me right here and now where am I trying to go? Just the usual remote reaction trying to record and document some random thoughts…. Did I?

The Power of Writing

Narrative No. 4
August 6, 2021

The power of writing is in a class of its own. I cannot think of a comparable one. Just to have that freedom of expression and thought, not only encourages your thought process, and allows for documentation, but sometimes delivers a message. What better means than to write and to gather and preserve. Somehow this all happens with me. I know not where this urge comes from or even the intent. Perhaps simply again the preservation of a special thought. Most always, I feel amazed to read my personal writing, perhaps with a subconsciousness of a specific intent or direction. Most likely so, judging from the random scattering of subject matter. All impromptu, even extemporaneously (I've been wanting to use that word forever) So here it all is, here and now. Try to explain even this random writing. It's simply a purging of the mind all allowing for a presentation of a thought or an impression of some kind, simply to allow for communicating on a convenient level, sometimes, all with the hope to express such. I seem to always be pleased with my expressions, perhaps wanting to share is the goal.

I feel the fiber of my being in many stories. Maybe sometimes even being absurd, irrelevant, maybe even incomprehensible, but it's all just me on my strange quest to write and express. Getting into this typing challenge is fun. It prompts me to read my own "writings", which for some strange reason, I hardly ever do. The intention with typing is to develop and preserve an orderly fashion of notes. The way I write is a mystery to me. I sincerely do not regard myself as a writer, professional or otherwise. Words just purge out, completely unplanned or premeditated, different topics and subject matter in different ways. All completely at random. Almost as a knee jerk reaction, then about an hour later, "ouija", three hundred words. Just moods, thoughts, expressions, and impressions are what I document. Some of which may seem non-sensible. But any part which may be meaningful, becomes my reward. Somewhere deep there is usually a message to be found. Just to uncover my messages and to discuss such, is rewarding for me. I've been known to be "silly", "salty" and sometimes arrogant. However, I must take a qualified exception to arrogant. Mr., Webster states: "full of or due to pride or haughty". Close but not all me, I accept haughty, the pride intent only to clarify with the closeness to my overall self-confidence, but never with any intent to offend. "Silly and salty" I accept only because that may be a component of my sense of humor. Usually kind of off the track, maybe even absurd with some oxymoron and some salt thrown in. But that's how I find my humor, I hope you take it.

My Quest

Back again and again trying hard to go on. Never intending to Give up. Just hoping I can somehow learn to type my own stories and not to be dependent on anyone. Anyone but I, and not to have to beg for help to type. This theoretical "book" of mine has unintentionally caused some dissention. Perhaps partially due to my basic expectations for others to react and oblige like I mostly do when called upon. But that's just a case of fantasizing, all wishful thinking. Now back to reality, I am here with Becky, my new laptop, and together we're ready to challenge the whole world, here and now. It might be most appropriate, in time to develop a short, dedicated narrative as a token of appreciation to my Tutini family, one and all. But here I am at this moment in time ready to take off, so let it be. Let me try to examine and try to understand about this phenomenon, computer thing, and certainly to understand my laptop, Becky. This is all very presumptuous on my part because I'm completely computer illiterate, shamefully. Really hiding for so many years,

only now to surface. Surface in a selfish way.
Me for my stories and my book.

A vain attempt for a legacy. Why not?
The intro to my book hinged on my memoirs,
what better way.? Most of my stories /narratives
are separate and unrelated perhaps enhancing
readers? However, you will find some common
subjects i.e. Life, Writing, Music, Spiritualism
and Love.

I characteristically take on fresh
thoughts which develop from a mood, into an
idea and most times into and hopefully into a
narrative with a message of some kind. It seems
most always to my personal satisfaction How
vain can one actually be? I celebrate an
impression. As an illustration on this past
Mother's Day, I composed a piece titled:
Momma, a very poignant collection of thought.
Me not being a Momma but most certainly a
Popa, may not truly qualify me. However, I have
a Momma in Heaven and truly a Momma she is.
That is my sole foundation to be so
presumptuous to write: Momma. A piece that
hopefully presents this overall miracle of life in
the true perspective of the leading character:
Momma. I will never tire or exhaust my reservoir
of admiration and respect for all mothers,
starting with my Love for my Wife and my Mom.

That is my guideline and inspiration for my tribute on Mother's Day. I'm confident my message is heard.

In a similar vein, we have "My Flag". This piece speaks entirely for itself. my tribute to the U.S.A.'s "Old Glory". Needless for me to go into similar depth as Momma. The ultimate basis here was to make a full presentation for my first book: "Find Your Rainbow, I Already Found Mine " Note the title double innuendo for finding your personal Rainbow in Life and perhaps even by your particular story selection and interest, you might find a rainbow there? My Rainbow.

Rain

Narrative No. 6
March 20, 2021

"Zoom" you open your umbrella - At the very first drop. Where does it come from? Somewhere from atop. Why is it here? It is hard to explain. Pitter-patter. Rain- such a lasting sound and feeling- makes you feel like reeling. Rain falling on the stretched umbrella. Any discomfort for getting or feeling wet, does not apply. Light out or dark it's almost the same. However, just slightly more soothing at night, in the rain. What comes from high creates a good feeling, "Rain". I'm not concerned with some chemical, geological or academic explanation. I just feel something special, the over-all kind of feeling, the chill, the wonder, the sensation of walking in rain and stepping in puddles is a delight of its own. You can hardly keep from dancing like "Singing in the Rain " until dawn. Kind of silly to point out this mood, somehow it feels refreshing. So, carry your umbrella even when it's dry. You never know what may fall from the sky.

Imagine

Narrative No. 7
May 12, 2020

Perhaps you may be looking at the remains of an ancient shipwreck on the rocky shore. The probable sun bleached wooden ribbed skeletal remains, along with a few rusted cannons, of what might have been a majestic ship long ago. Let's say a sailing ship, as possible. That thought of the mighty masted master, the total of which along with cannons, places her into a special category of size and purpose. Let's name her as the "Lousiea".

See the anxious sails and halyards unfurled and blowing in the wind. The cosmetic feature of a defined anchor secured to the forward hull side. The intricate beauty of the body hull, designed and built to defy and sustain the full and complete wrath of the ocean. And in turn allowing for the calm graceful cutting through the white waves. The vessel being propelled in the sea by soaring winds in the sails. The navigational control with the rudder astern and working placement of the sails all allowing for direction, for steerage and sailing to the best advantage.

Alarmingly, the lashing winds suddenly start howling, blowing, and ripping at the sails with the waves beating and washing at the gunwales, the surprising instant helplessness of it all, and now the ultimate sorrowful thought that this fine being of a vessel, with whatever flag waving, may now become as a crashed wreckage on the pernicious rocks, and to imagine the human panic that was above and below. Maybe even while searching for the missing lighthouse "Beacon". Along with the desperate deck gun volley as a cry for help. All toll a very sorry sight but a happening that can even correlate to certain surprisingly sudden turning moments and experiences in ordinary life.

Imagine cargo spilling out and being wasted, along with possibly the added expense of human life. All this pictured and thought of by just viewing lonely, abandoned pieces of wreckage on the rocky beach. And to realize the thousands of rainfalls and relentless wave beatings as having been imposed. Sunrise and sunset into such now serenity.... As sometimes in our present thoughts.

Such an exercise, to take a peaceful scene and to make it into a moment of intensity and interest, casually by playing with words, and winds, like putting a pencil to a sketch with a similar effort of creativity and ultimate end effect. Stimulate the imagination even if only now with thoughts and along with the word depiction possibly having striking emotions and revelations.

Similarly, even the making of music with sounds that can reach such profound pitch, point of expression then crescendo, like a storm. And with similar excitement, and then suddenly stillness. This causal narrative was an intended effort to present an impressionable scenario: "calm" to the "hectic" and then to the desperate end as "peaceful and serene. "Just Imagine if you can.......?

The Book

Narrative No. 8
June 18, 2021

I'm nearing completion of my very first book. A very exciting thought to share here and now. I did not ever imagine I would or even could do so. There are many great books that justify being so. Some great novels, (too numerous to mention) fiction, nothing wrong with fiction. I personally happen to like fiction. I have known some intellectuals (some being writers of their own) who frown on fiction, as a lower level of writing. To me that's unjust. My position to any of them would simply be to explore the different avenues and values that authors in this category of writing may offer. So many ways to appreciate a book. Almost, unlikely that I can do so here and now. However, I take this brief opportunity to express my own private thoughts about books and writing. Where did this all start? A good and rather interesting question. Maybe on a leaf? Certainly, on some parchment, or even carved in stone. Let's not overlook Hieroglyphics, perhaps thousands of years ago, time factor of no matter here for us right now.

My first story came as somewhat of a surprise to me. It all started on New Year's Eve Dec. 31, 2019. Really not that long ago but became the actual start of my writing quest. Very presumptuous for me to believe that my "writing" has any worth or merit but to me personally, yes. I feel good about my stories, I even have a feeling of comfort to think I may have created something of interest for my own family at the very least, And maybe perhaps to a few others.

Sharing thoughts, being the basic incentive for a book to become the fun part of writing. The very thought (for me for example) is that I may be able to communicate with many others. Not to sell or promote, simply to share, such as here and now. Other uses can be such as " door stop" "paper weight" as a " step up". Not to be facetious. First off, we all know the title is important, important so as to attract the reader. Something catchy, to lure you in. Naturally something indicative of the story and subject matter itself. Stay with fiction for now. Nonfiction etc. We may get to later. So much to consider upon your selection. First and quite naturally the interest in the basic category of choice. Such as mystery, or murder mystery, for example. The suspense thru-out or the reason or to "solve " the happening. So many categories to suggest. That is not the purpose of these narratives. I guess my purpose is to create an advantage to examine my own reasons and methods to communicate along with various thoughts and impressions. This book being my first attempt, and experiencing some accomplishment and some pride in myself, just at the very thought that it would even be possible for me. And just by putting these thoughts and emotions down in writing no way makes me a writer. No pretenses here. In fact, I've written separate pieces on that matter. One big reward for me is to be able to read my own stuff. And most often I find it enjoyable, and challenging. The surprise and pleasure to be fascinated, and that this is at all possible for me becomes my engine and comfort to think that # 1 I even tried, and # 2 I may have even succeeded. I cannot honestly justify my attempt at all this. All kind of strange, puzzling and even mysterious.

Why now? What for at this late stage of my life? Who knows? Not me. All I truly can account for is my very first attempt. That being: "A Christmas Story". (Here Narrative No. 32) Such an easy and loving subject. Not intended as a mere casual subject for story and skirting the meaning of CHRISTMAS Which is an endearing subject for all time. So, upon my ultimate completion, I shall take pride and comfort to enjoy this experience, which for me is a truly surprising feat. Note: book title having been carefully chosen as the double innuendo being to find your rainbow in life or perhaps in this narrative array of various subject matter. Just as a passing point of, perhaps interest relating to the subject of reading. I casually estimate that I have read about 600 books in my lifetime, not including textbooks, newspapers, magazines or my music. This would represent my 46.6-ounce brain having processed approximately 42 million words plus the 25000 plus words here in this book. Not bad. And the night is still young. Perhaps this could be an incentive and excuse for my next book?

High Rise

Narrative No. 9
July 22, 2021

So, you want to build a "High Rise". Let us be the General Contractor. The appropriate beginning naturally being layout involving surveying etc. excavation, foundation, into superstructure. Layout to be continuous through-out. Foundations as a separate entity. This will vary in many ways. But basically, as the bottom support for the upper phase known as superstructure.

Now to the features of reinforced concrete [may we use "R.C. for ease] the reinforcement as steel rods known as "rebars" for the tension requirement for strength. Now the concrete works in compression. Tension and compression are the two conditions in which R.C. works. Works as in actual support structurally.

The concrete to be made up of cement, sand, coarse aggregate, [such as crushed stone or gravel] water and admixtures [as may be required under certain circumstances]. The design mix as defined by the strength requirements. This is all part of the basic structural design. Strengths are defined as p.s.i., [pounds per square inch] this can be such as 2500psi, 3000, psi, and up. A basic structure [coming on the foundation below] can consist of columns [as vertical members] beams, and arches[slabs] all integral with each other. The joining of which makes for the structure.

Now to say our hypothetical building is 30 stories high and 16000 square feet per floor. This we will do as the basis for this narrative. Fundamentally the columns support the beams and the now the fun part.

The formwork involved to create this R.C. floor slab. Logically the forms are built to shape and accommodate the placement of the concrete mix. Most always the concrete strength requirement will vary. Columns being higher than beams and slab. Here we'll suppose Columns at 4000 psi and beams at 3500 psi. And that will be the pattern of placement. Sequencing naturally being columns then beams with floor slab.

Placement must be monolithic. That to be as one. Absolute placement to be continued to allow the R.C. to become a working structure all to satisfy design criterion, No interruption in the placement under any circumstances. In the process of placement Vibrators are used to vibrate the concrete still In its plasticity state allowing for the vibrator to distribute the mix thoroughly the aggregates with the cement etc.

The correct proportions of the mix as a separate design of its own to develop the required strength. Water being a critical component. Must be precise to allow plasticity for placement but too much will weaken the structure. The cast in place procedure is under a strict degree of inspection (by a licensed lab) also inspection at the batching plant. High control at base of delivery by procedure of "slump test" This consists of a cone shaped cylinder and rodding of testing sample all to substantiate correctness of plasticity. In addition to test cylinders made for lab testing to substantiate correct strengths per design requirements all by qualified inspectors. The reinforcement being circular, deformed, steel bars of varying diameters giving for different tensional strength, all determined by design requirements. Overall concept for building based on many requirements by owner or client. Starting with excavation and foundation to be treated as a separate entity. In the course of placing the redi-mix concrete the arch [or slab] is to be screeded by cement masons to a level of finish floor elevation. Progressively as the concrete starts to cure [harden] the cement masons trowel the floor surface to a smooth finish. Key here is the precise timing for steel troweling. Correct elevation and overall layout to be controlled and marked out by layout engineers, As previously stated "layouts continuous and ongoing. Critical to overall correctness of structure. As to square level and plumbness. The formwork done by carpenters. Beam and column forms prefabricated. Entire deck area [plywood] forms supported by a system of jacks and posts. As the weight off the labs. All as designated on shop drawings. All allowing for fabrication and placement of column and beam rebars. All allowing other trades i.e. plumbers, electricians, heating and ventilating contractors and any other trade requiring items and sleeves embedded in the concrete. The electrician is most always the most prevalent here. As it is most economical to run conduit in the slab as later in the hung ceilings. All this done in coordination with the progress of the forming etc.

The control for sequencing of form stripping as designated in the specifications. Also, with weather conditions. Also, some test cylinders as cast by inspectors are designated to substantiate the actual degree of strength attained. This at usually a three-day curing period. Upon attaining a required strength, the stripping of forms can be done. A temporary jack support system is provided to help support forms, rebars and ready-mix concrete is substantial. All formwork with lateral support bracing, the new slab system. Continuity for continuing forming upper floor construction is important and necessary to maintain a cycle of production and progress. The feasibility for our hypothetical 16000 s.f. floor area is to be done in 4 separate quadrants. Lending to logistical cycling continuity. As for winter weather procedures there are many factors involved i.e. admixtures to accelerate curing to defer concrete from freezing, temporary heat with absolute enclosure, and more. It is to be said quite naturally, all aspects of work done in full compliances of Bldg. Dept. Code and all other agencies having jurisdiction. The hoisting provisions assist in all phases of construction, including formwork, rebars, concrete placement, and for all other trades and activities.

Here you now have your High-Rise superstructure, complete and ready to follow with all the many, many other activities to become a complete and finished building. Are you sure you want to build a "High Rise"?...........Let's Go!............

Mitsu… Phew

Narrative No. 10
May 1, 2021

Here's a chuckle for today. My Mitsubishi has this strange odor and noise from the AC unit. Domenique contends it smells like a dead mouse. Jio confirmed and ordered a new compartment air filter. Dom also complained about dust shooting out of the vents into her eyes. Here is my response to her:

Dust is bad and may even cause a head-on collision. Then the mouse odor may no longer matter. When your entire body is in a cast, you are in traction, on two I V's, with plasma (Type A), oxygen, and an EKG in progress, and the Priest giving "Last Rights" then maybe the mouse odor can be tolerable. We ordered the filter anyway. It is probably refundable if you don't "make it".

Runs Better Clean

Narrative No. 11
May 10, 2021

Car, Auto, Wheels- Such an important part of your life. No longer a luxury but an absolute necessity. The basic wheel development probably started out of stone then to wood, then to a jump to tubeless white wall radials. A great phenomenon. Along with the wagon development several hundred years ago. The wagon was a prevalent factor in the development of this country and worldwide going back to who knows where or when?

But back to your car, your "pet" and your special feeling towards it. It's truly amazing what the car has come to mean in this present life, and present world. This present day in time the car has become in a class by itself. Maybe in a similar category to the cell phone. Amazing how dependent we became on both. There are certainly other similar categories of interest, but I just randomly chose your car today.

Naturally owning two cars at the present time perhaps qualifies me to present this commentary for no special reason, other than perhaps as a literary exercise and possible subject of interest. Be that as it may, I am certain that most readers will relate. Your car is just a personal, intimate possession that is almost representative of you. Color is pertinent, always a meaningful choice. Or perhaps just fate or some happenstance a color that we end up with, no matter.

But we gas them without hesitation almost like the necessity of feeding a hungry child and usually even feel privileged, particularly with the return of service. Out in the rain blistering sun and snow. Uncomplaining, just always there to serve you. Good days and bad days, all requiring care and attention including regular maintenance. This is all part of the relationship. Complaints hardly ever, maybe a "won't start" as an occasional message but that's considered fair.

Wash it occasionally let it shine'
Runs better clean, right?

Bottled Water

Narrative No. 12
August 6, 2021

"Water, water everywhere and not a drop to drink ". The sudden craze for water came on big time. Stop to think and to realize the history of drinking water. As far back in time as can be imagined, man simply scooped up with both hands his drink, from the well river or the creek, without much effort, thousands and thousands of years ago. Done naturally simply to satisfy a thirst.

How easy and convenient it hardly required even a thought. Drinking water is an important ingredient for existence and survival. A major factor for body functions. Developed quite naturally with the use also of leaves, shells, skins and any form of container available, by natural convenience.

Not at that primitive time requiring or providing deposit or return. Coming by evolution to today's water bottle phenomenon. A giant industry grew almost overnight, it seems. This being very beneficial for all. Water being most essential for body hydration. Now everywhere and everyone can be seen with this prolific bottle in their hand, plastic or otherwise. Absolutely essential for life existence.

The surge came on gradually perhaps starting here in the U.S. during World War 2. Not to say bottled water wasn't in use prior, it certainly was. Just that now the lifestyle may prompt people to be more conscious of their bodies' demand for a drink. This review focuses mainly on water. Certainly, the convenient containers and all forms of bottling lent to today's development of casual drinking water everywhere. And how, this did so most certainly to encourage and allow for this necessary means of hydration.

This subject presentation is basically rather dull to convey but could be made interesting in many aspects. Think of the psychological demand imposed on most all: young, old, tall, short, man and woman. Everyone has developed this need, this desire, this craves, this dependency on drinking water, morning, noon and night. Most beneficial for a healthy body functional system. Even in the military it is mandatory by way of the water canteen on the belt at all times. Helps even an army to always be healthy and fit.

Such a giant industry was born and developed with big monetary profits made. And coupled with providing massive employment globally: All with bottling, trucking, distribution, sales and cashing in your 5-cent deposit, another newborn business establishment. Also, to realize a nuisance factor with all those massive piles of empty bottles accumulating and piling up. Overwhelming as a competitive form of everyday KLUTTER. However, the potential revenue returns (your own money) are good here. People need water, want water and people have water.

Now as a Norman Rockwell scene we have the water bottle in hand. No complaints or criticism here, just a commentary review of man's progress. Moon shots, computers, age of electronics. Most certainly to include your cell phone, (which is fodder for another story). All to everyone's' benefit the water bottle is here to stay. Enjoy the varieties, but mostly the physical gain benefits and not to forget the 5-cent refund.

Everyone, all parts of the population. Doctors, Lawyers, Indian Chiefs and upon close look even probably our own Statue of Liberty. Cheers, Salute, Skool. Everyone was all with bottles in their hands. All dull and uninteresting? Then why is it you have that 5-cent shell or leaf in your hand? So much fun.

Even Santa Claus needs hydration, Mrs. Santa too. "Equal Rights' "as some important footnotes passed down in the ancient hieroglyphics and time. Back to the early recount of "The hand scoop in the river. " It's preferable for hands to be clean. Must be politically correct at all times. And also remember to be timely with all refunds on leaves and shells. And also, to note, leaves and shells besides being refundable are also to be recyclable.

Pearls

Narrative No. 13
August 9,2021

But I mean to give you "Pearls", certainly not a "Nothing Burger" on an "Everything Roll". And I've been known to play with the English language. But sometimes when I may be grammatically incorrect, it's intentional and for a purpose. The intent here with my narratives is to share some inner-most thoughts and feelings. Be them as they may, some casual and some somewhat deep. And some overwhelmingly, incomprehensibly, incoherent. But so what? Nobody's perfect.

Contemplation

Narrative No. 14
September 16, 2021

This narrative is not intended to be affiliated with some other narratives, maybe only around the edges. This now represents fresh commentary on old thoughts. Looking back with a lot to think about. Centering around regrets (a sensitive category) it is normal to have regrets and to think about it. Sure you, coulda, woulda, shoulda, but you didn't always, maybe things just happen the way it was meant to be? But what about here and now? Regrets? That could be heavy baggage. Some thoughts are not so easy to dismiss. You can tell yourself you did the best you could, if that's so, so be it. Too late to think otherwise.

Whatever, however, the race continues even as we grow older. Would you now like to do it over? It doesn't work that way. There shall be a reckoning in your own heart and mind. No harm to think about some things now, why not take that step back? See where you've been, where you are, and where you might be going. Take stock. Can you change anything past? Not likely. Can you just think about possible redirection? Not to an extreme but take hold here and now. Confront any potential regret if that is at all possible. Yes, maybe redirection but not within the category of regret.

Just step back and take a good look. Right now, it is still within your power to do things right, which is most likely your direction anyway. Take this moment to think and see the full picture (now a wonderful opportunity) is there room for change or reconsideration. Or can this all be unnecessary thought, as you may be on the golden track right now. Certainly, it's all what you want anyway. You may always intend and want to do the right thing but sometimes it's not just like some happy coincidence, and still things don't always work out favorably. You are in charge of your own life. Live within your own character, your ethics, and your conscience. You are certainly not intending to do wrong.

However, life is not always that simple. Just to walk out the door and to meet your day may become a challenge at times. But not to develop any fears or phobias, at this or at any point in life. The world is your "Oyster", for you to be happy and thankful, forgiving and also loving. Be yourself and don't take this

"Contemplation" so seriously. You continue to do your best. You can live with that and to know where you are, with all this potential to continue to do the right thing and to do good and believe in it all as so certainly not to cloak yourself in regrets………..What A Wonderful Life! Right this very moment. Don't lose sight of it.

Pause

Narrative No. 15
March 31, 2021

What we have done with our lives, (to date) is done and gone, even yesterday. Now what we do with our future, is what is now of primary importance and of concern. Starting today this very moment, know all the opportunities are here, here if you want them. Be sure of your wants, mix up a few dreams and fantasies. You're entitled.

Dreams and wishes are exciting. Try to keep it close to real. Remember you can't go back. Back maybe in the nature of a memory. The intent here was never to take that away. That past is primarily the foundation of your life and soul and what has helped shape your character. This is all good and allows you to go on strongly. Here is your brand-new day. Take it and do what you want with it. Just think tomorrow today will become yesterday, also to be gone.

Simply thinking, take this opportunity to do some good for yourself or for another. Whatever may come along, let's stay with ourselves for now. How selfishly do we use this day? That's OK, we already said we're entitled.

Do something with fun, do something happy, do something kind, do something dutifully. See such a vast horizon, and we're only focusing, and contemplating one day. Imagine the vast potential and promise of the rest of your life. So much to do. Do much that can be done for yourself and others. Start with now, today! Think of what might please you most. As a starter, call an olde time friend, and catch up on lost time. Make some definite plans together. Do the shopping you've been wanting to do. Tend to bills and business you've been hiding from. But now better still, be with a loved one, you can feel your heart beating faster already. Get the message? Also, family, most always a priority, always in a tender loving way. Never do it as a burdensome chore or unwanted responsibility. Take your brand-new day and ENJOY.

Seek and Thou Shall Find

Narrative No. 16
October 17, 2021

I know for certain that loneliness can be sad and even depressing, but for sure everyone must have something to be thankful for, so let's build on that whatever it might be. It's a start just make yourself content and know that it is within your power to conquer this thing called loneliness, this takes true strength of mind and heart. Push the loneliness away. You are here right now giving it a shove. Feel comfortable with what you have, make it real and it will grow. I'm sure you can make it all happen and you may even lend a friend some confidence and comfort to give them a lift. Why not?

We are basically each as an individual sole being. We are alone within ourselves. Yes family, loved ones, friends, acquaintances, the butcher, the baker, the candlestick maker. All together but we as sole bodied individuals are basically alone. This becomes maybe almost your choice. Think hard about this. Whatever your status is right now you are somewhat satisfied with it. Let me address this piece to those ones that are truly alone. I say again most likely by your choice. You may be ambivalent about this but there must be some possible means of adjustment here. Granted there are many people that truly want it this way: "Loners" That's' OK you are entitled. This is your life; I just want to analyze things and maybe inspire or get to say things that you may feel and start to think about. This is a harmless chat.

My intent is to see if I do find any that don't want to be alone but find themselves so. Give this deep thought and be honest with yourself. We shall analyze this subject and perhaps reveal some innermost secret feelings. I believe this will be truly beneficial to a few. Even to me, just to have this one opportunity to perhaps help, advise or guide someone, anyone in need.

A long day alone. A lonely day alone. You do manage to pass the day, but that's exactly what we're getting at, to help make the day meaningful, such a tall order. However, above all remember to never neglect family, they need you and you need them, Family will most always give you comfort, support and most importantly, LOVE.

Always smile and always make eye contact with others, Smile and promote a greeting to all, including, likely strangers. If you have a pet, that's great, then you're not alone-alone. Get a nice plant, nurture it and talk to it.

Always know the name of the person you are speaking to, even the cashier. This always brightens every situation. And makes your day better. Never hesitate for a light compliment, when appropriate, it makes you and others feel good to create a pleasant moment. Keep in touch, don't lock yourself down. Encourage a friendship. Very likely you may have a lonely friend or even acquaintance. Build a friendship, you may need each other. Share your time, mutual interests and thoughts, and find some fun. This may not be so possible, but it could be a start. This entire scenario is vast and infinite but certainly not hopeless.

We shall continue to analyze loneliness as a very important matter. With enough thought and effort, we can certainly arrive at some good ideas and plans. You can start to feel better right now, because this is possible and not hopeless. We are all human and do have the ability to help ourselves and even perhaps help others with similar needs. Feeling better already? START YOUR DAY WITH A SMILE-...........Kisses later.!

Is That All There Is?

Narrative No. 17
May 27th, 2021

The good outweighs the bad. That may be one reason why we are here, to experience both. But let the good be as good as it can be. This is what helps us make it through the day and make it through life. A strong mind with strong faith. Sure, you want "it all" why not? But it's not meant to be that way. We're here for a short time and our blueprint is fair and just, we must see it that way. We must always count our blessings and that must be enough, because that's all there is. Take it and enjoy life the way you should. Keep all your love and faith in your heart forever and forever is a long time.

Precious Moments

Narrative No. 18
February 7, 2021

Life is here right now, right this very moment. Let us know that and think of all the times yet to come, good times and maybe some bad times. The good times are what count. Time to enjoy all and to be remembered and saved. But to keep knowing this is this the real time, each day- each year. Look back too, look back and think of all the past, all those precious moments to remember. Gone, but not forgotten.

Let us make it now, these times, good times not only to reflect and reminisce, but to enjoy life right now. Enjoy in your natural way with faith in your loved ones and friends.

Just a short trip, but we will live on. Live on with legacies, and other's memories. We take this opportunity to appreciate life, with every breath. Each day- a new day with new adventures.

Keep your mind and your heart open - open to faith and open to love. Make it known to others with affection and caring. Make it known to yourself that you did good when you had the opportunity. This moment here and now is your opportunity. Share your love. It's all real.

The Circle of Life

Narrative No. 19
August 14, 2021

The spirit of this narrative is reflected as in many other stories here. With family, your very being from cradle to grave, that's what it's meant to be. But what's meant to be, may not be enough for you. Read my "Momma, my Fathers' Day Tribute, and my Flag" and a few others. Get the feel, part of the fiber of life. You can sense the messages and my direction. What good are all these "messages"? It all starts with the heart. Naturally with the mind as back-up. And for the full scenario, we're all entitled with faith with our own individual views and values. This includes our own lives, to be said as: "My Way". This to be within certain guidelines and certain parameters. All to allow ultimately for a peaceful and loving life. Make your breakthrough right now to stop and realize what life is really all about. You're not in the circle, you're riding the circle. Simple it's all been programmed. All with the best of plans and intentions. Always understand the right way. This should almost be natural. We All have our own inner-most thoughts, and feelings; goals to be earned. Earned in many ways. Live a believing loving, caring, honest and respectful life. And always remember: "To Thine Our Own Self Be True".

All is not easy. All good things require faith, effort and certainly The Blessing to arrive at the "good" spots. Arrive, appreciate and enjoy. Round and round with our circle, on the merry-go-round of life. Always trying to grab the "Brass Ring". Don't let life pass you by. Enjoy all the love and happiness that you deserve. And when you're "there" know it, you're in the sweet spot of life, along with all your loved ones and caring friends. It's not that clearly defined as you're living it. Unfortunately, it's sometimes realized late.

To look back and know those very moments as good times and heart-warming. But when it's all gone. Feel not grief and sorrow, but with thankfulness for your special being, all with cherished memories. But now take this time to realize more "sweet spots" to be had and to be lived. You're here now, put this tapestry together and enjoy. All good, make it all good just the way it should be.

All you need now and always is believing in yourself and faith. It's all there with-in you, life from day one up to this very moment. Make good things happen and enjoy your "Circle of Life". Rainbows will be your legacy.

My Soliloquy

Narrative No. 20
April 24, 2020

Sure, your body weakens when you get on, but you must keep a strong mind. It will make a difference allowing you to do what you choose and what you may have yet to do.

Continue to read a good book, write, play your music, laugh, have fun, keep the sink clean, that's a part of it. Just important to be able to do as you please. Don't ever put yourself in a compromising position or the wrong place. Keep your mind, spirit and body safe, confident, comfortable and stable.

When senior and "Golden Years' do ' come- you shall have paid your dues. Just enjoy ... try keeping things simple and uncomplicated. " "Be as happy as you make up your mind to be" (credit to Abe Lincoln).

Quiet and lost days that's all a part of living. Can't hit a "Grand Slam" every day. So, what. Enjoy- Life and whatever...

You've got it all- Life, Loved Ones and Family. Still breathing and still able to care. Don't make your own aneurysms. Make it easy- try harder to Just Enjoy.

Pain

Narrative No. 21
August 9, 2021

This is mainly applicable to me and any other poor souls suffering.

I like pain. It helps remind me to appreciate the time when I'm feeling good. We always take the good times for granted without even a thought, why should we? Health and wellbeing, such a blessing. Just going through life thinking it's a bed of roses. Sorry for you upon your awakening. Pain can sometimes be unbearable, like right now. What to do? Prayers are sure to help, but sometimes not enough, certainly not tonight. Now the challenge is to sleep. The chance to hide from the "demon", I hope, Tomorrow will tell, what to do?

Pain, never the right time or even the wrong time. Bare it somehow. It still hurts, just to ease up a bit, perhaps enough to sleep? What a wonderful thought, the avenue of escape. No moment of ease, why? So hard to understand, it's just that time, the time to suffer a bit, more than a bit. There's a lot of suffering and pain going on out there, so why complain? Because it hurts, hurts constantly, disallowing me from doing hardly anything.

Sometimes just brushing my teeth becomes an entity. But you manage. Perhaps it may ease up. Don't despair, wait for tomorrow, can't get much worse, Getting soft? Not so very long-ago things would be trivial, trivial where it would just feel natural and expected. Now things are somewhat different, nothing is trivial anymore. What good to complain or dote? Move on don't focus so hard, it's only PAIN. See you when I see you, I hope. Get those prayers going and fast.

Three Pounds, Five Ounces

Narrative No. 22
August 19,2021

Three Pounds Five Ounces is all she weighed. She came to us that one Friday. Our Christmas was filled with joy and delight, when Santa saw her that night.

What miracles God does create, allowing us all our blessings, somethings we may very well deserve. And here we are with our just serve. We named her Karen, and right from the start, she stole our hearts. How can you resist her with her smile so bright when you love her with all you might? Two more at home who we must fit into this poem. A brother and a sister, who could also not resist her. She fit right in, just like a pin. What a wonderful gift from God. We're all in awe the more we saw her grow. And for us to know that she belonged here with us and for us not to fuss, just watch her in wonder. And not put asunder the blessing bestowed and always to know that she is ours to keep and never to weep that we found our lost sheep.

And now she grew up and we still look in awe, and look all around, now that we found a life that can be like a dream. All because of this

"Preem "that's now part of our scene. To have and to hold and always be told, to thank God for our little blessing.

This as a Tribute and Thanks to my wife Virginia for Our 10 week Precious "Preemie".

Seventy-Five Days and Seventy-Four Nights

Narrative No. 23
August 28, 2021

A journey of convalescence. Never has a daughter's love for a father been more present and pronounced. Always a sensitive scenario, when a "visitor" may invade the privacy of one's home. The father is far from just a visitor. However, it is still an intrusion. But love conquers all. She dotes, and serves, treats, cares for and loves. You would never ask for this and in today's world and never expect it. But where does it come from? This phenomenon, coupled with love and respect. It comes from upbringing and a good family life.

The father cannot help feeling as a burden. But not so, he is made to feel as if he belongs there. A 24\7 job for a loving daughter who makes it known and apparent to feel privileged to serve. All the way: supervision of medication, oxygen, meals, snacks, back rubs, nebulizer, eye drops, shower and toiletry scheduling, foot rubs, body creams, hair brushing, bedding, laundry, constant care and doctor office visits, also to sleep with one eye open and an ear to the door. Requiring more than care for a newborn infant. More than a full-time job: a full-time responsibility all done completely, responsibly and uncomplainingly. Such a display of love, respect, devotion all and more. It would not be fair to make such a burden and imposition on anyone almost under any circumstances.

The daughter has other family responsibilities and also to attend to her own personal self. The father feels greatly appreciative, but with such reservation so as to dominate someone's own life. Where do we go from here, the nearest nursing home? That might very well be the fair alternative.
Tribute to my Loving daughter, Karen.

K For Klutter

Narrative No. 24
April 24th, 2021

Today is Saturday, a quiet kind of a day. For some reason I always seem to have grandiose ideas of doing so many things. Things that are not usually important but kind of stuck in your mind. But some things are important and must be done, done in a timely manner. The big iceberg that waits patiently to surface is KLUTTER. It's always there not necessarily hiding but definitely growing exponentially. Almost like it's breathing and breeding.

I regard this as "spontaneous generation". A scientific term that is well suited for self-reproduction. When it gets away from you and you completely lose control, now this becomes serious. This monster captivates you and your home, growing and growing right before your very eyes. Drawers, closets, countertops, tabletops, shelving, and all over. Not only does it restrict and deny fair usage of space, it's burdensome, unsightly and even depressing. The entire scenario is absurd. The bulk of this creature matters as a problem. (Let's) just refer to it, as "K", for you know what.

Now "K" has got you locked in and nowhere to move. Sad, very sad, but why? Also how, when, and for what reason? Get back to the why? Why? Because you let it happen. When "K" really spreads and takes over and you lose even floor space, and now have to step over things. This becomes completely out of control, and we haven't even mentioned garages, attics, basements, and perhaps you may even have escalated to paid storage space!

What to do at this point? And this "point" is most likely now. Right now. Look around, what do you see," K" ......It almost defies you in an obscene way. How can you even imagine all this actually occurring and truly being, but there it is looking right at you? Perhaps even laughing at you. Not sure this is a laughing matter. In fact, it is almost a crying matter. Unfortunately, this "K" business is a common problem. What to do? What to do?.......I don't really know.

I'm stuck here "growing" myself. Maybe you can start by cutting off the "supply" however possible and render major restrictions and restraints accordingly. Limit the flow some-what, but what to do with all that's nested? This has grown BIG. Unfortunately, it is too big. Start now to focus. Get to the overflowing impassable, almost impossible areas. Let's start with counter-tops, a very essential area to be accessible. Just start cleaning like you mean it and mean it! Get that done and this program may continue?

Tacit Tuesday

Narrative No. 25
July 24th, 2021

Tuesday, sadly lacking any recognition or glory. However, the basic calendar was prepared just as well. There may have been suspicion that Tuesdays wouldn't quite make it. Mind you this is only 2021.Tuesday has made it this far, thru earthquakes, wars, hurricanes, depressions, blazing sun. revolutions, famine, pandemics, industrial revolution, automobile, moon shots, inflations' recessions, strikes, electronic age, creation of disposable diapers, TV commercials, Aluminum siding, and many more trying times.

All the other days have their own highlights. Start with Wed., the day after Tues. Now you have made mid-week, starting to feel better, particularly after getting away from Tues. Wed. an easy comfortable day knowing the weekend is really not that far away. Relax, the weekend is coming. Bad things don't usually happen on Weds., just mind crossing on the green and not in-between, don't walk under any ladders, watch out for black cats not to cross your path and keep your fingers and toes crossed all day. You'll be fine. Most likely you'll make it.

Wait to awaken Thursday. Morning to be sure. Now here's your Thursday. The best feature is you made it this far and tomorrow is Fri. Undoubtedly almost the best day of the week. Don't forget it's "get-a-way day", so wear your sneakers for the running start.

Even if you may be home sick in bed with a fever, remember tomorrow's The Big Day. OK you made it. You awaken with a calm excitement; you don't want to spoil this special day: Friday. Of course, the sun is shining and you're ready. This day is a relaxed kind of a day, kind-a easy to make it fun. Easy even if you're a window washer on the Empire State Bldg. with the hic-cups, or working in the zoo cleaning the elephant cage, or in the Fulton Fish Market and you forgot your deodorant. You're still content with the thought of Sat. Coming up. Now you made it, certainly Tues is long gone and forgotten.

Ok, Saturday is here. Perhaps a chance to sleep in. But only the theoretical day of rest. However, this is the time for laundry, food shopping, paying bills, and house cleaning. And stripping the beds, haircut or salon, dog to the vet or to be groomed. When Mom's cooking you can wash the cars, clean the gutters, trim the lawn and hedges, clean the garage, pick-up at the cleaners, give the kid a driving lesson (sneak in lunch). Have supper, read the newspaper and then relax to enjoy your day off.

Sunday, really the best day of the week. Big breakfast, early Services, some more newspaper, meal preparations, eating early, a couple of phone calls, cleaning the litter box, then visiting Grandma and Grandpa, home at last, maybe a little snack. Already getting "The Big Chill "? That's "Blue Monday " knocking at the door. Try hard to relax and enjoy the quiet tranquil Sunday evening. You're in the comfort of your own home, pay no attention to that knocking at the door, there's no one there. It's just that "chill". Beddy Bye.

Ok Monday wins, to Sunday. Here it comes like a locomotive into the station. Get up now it's here, no more knocking at the door, which knocking is in your head. The shower is your only chance, take it you've got a 50/50 chance of making it. Pick a nice suit, you may need it. Quick breakfast, a kiss at the door and" Varoom ", on your way.

Tough to get the Monday started, the "wheels' ' have been stopped for 64 hours, no problem," wheels" are back turning again, looking good. Next, back to our low-keyed Tues. right where this all began. Only to tell again of poor Tuesday, always being quiet, insignificant, lonely, completely unacknowledged and uncelebrated, but it's there on the calendar so live it and embrace it as any other day in your life, because it's there. We kind of skimmed our Thursday because Thursday is a casual day. It's such an easy-going day knowing you're on the shirttails of glamorous Friday.... Not to worry about Thursday, it already passed.

Tuesday did well with more than 700 words. We really like Tuesdays, although it's just a day without much spark, and most always gets confused with Wednesdays. But remember it's still a precious day in your life to enjoy.......... Correction 693 words not 700, there goes Tuesday again, looking for false recognition. Wait till Friday finds out.

Fun

Narrative No. 26
May 10, 2021

Fun comes and then goes. I don't know exactly where it goes and what's to take its place. Fun is not necessary to define. However, it is necessary to enjoy it. It differs with many other happenings. You are to make your own pleasures, that's not to say that fun is not always there, and ready at the right time and the right place. It is pleasurable with Mr. Webster. therefore, it must be. Go and find it, enjoy it.

Oftentimes when in the midst, you're not truly conscious of it, fun that is. When you do reflect it is fun, fun that may go unrecognized as such. But when it's all but gone you savor the little bit that's left or comes around. Enjoying a moment or something memorable. Just wonderful to realize that those good times were really there. So natural in it's happening, like that's exactly the way it should be.

But now upon reflecting it grows dim. But once it was all real, just to note the good times in your life. Now to live with those thoughts, and the memories that allow you to endure. Endure what? Life as it inevitably evolves. It's just that now your fun is not the same.

Now the word "fun" takes on a more subdued mood. You almost must help create or will it with your own mind, heart and spirit. Mostly with the help of having known the real thing. So, take what you now have and enjoy.

Fun may not be the prime motivator for a moment, but it certainly may become a delightful side effect. 322 words to tell you that fun is pleasurable. That you are having fun and you may not even know it.

Cynical: defines as: sarcastic, sneering, denying the sincerity of a happening, and or, people's motives and actions. Is that what my little narrative does? It's not meant to.

Momma

Momma...Five letters, not much, but everything. Everything that truly matters. Matters to who? Should matter to you, right now. All living things have or had Mommas. Dinosaurs, Crocodiles, Bengal Tigers, even Elephants yes and even me and you. Where does it start? Upon conception starting right that very moment she starts serving you, and it never really stops. The love and the caring and all that goes with it.

This is not a story, certainly as a story is expected to be. This is my heart on this page. Not just a piece of it, but all of it and then all again and again.

Leave the lions, tigers, and bears for now and open your own heart. Do you remember? Should not take any effort at all, it's all there in your heart. In a very special spot. Hurts now, why? Why because it may be gone and there's nothing, nothing to compare to a mother and her love. Money, material possessions and even "certain others "can never take the place of Momma.

A Mother dedicates her entire life and being to her child. No limits, no compromises. Purely and completely unconditional. Let us accept that as fact. Now long after the womb, her work still goes on. On with a great deal of sacrificing mentally and physically to beyond extremes.

Being male it's not easy to comprehend all this phenomenon that's happening, but it all is happening. Upon a grueling childbirth experience, now it kind of begins at the next stage. With some cases of breast feeding, it is so natural for the baby right from the start. To be receiving and depending on Momma completely. It is not possible to make this presentation complete in any way. We will try to. On to the bathing, feeding, caring (24/7 plus), let's not forget the fun diaper part. All this is routine in a sense of becoming mandated, necessary and yes critical to our precious treasure. All with uncompromising love. Love, another short word with a long meaning.

Things may start to get boring to all but Momma, Momma's too busy to get bored. In fact, with no time to hardly care for her own personal being, wants, and needs. Baby comes first above all others. The past womb stage is also part of this miracle of life, the miracle that really never ends. A Mother's dedication and love compares to nothing else. Amazing how the offspring expects all of it in such a natural unquestionable manner. Mommas supposed to feed, protect, care, teach, clean, provide, love, and show love.

Start with care; it is all-inclusive, to fondle, attend to, look after, yes and even play. All as teaching and guiding. How can you possibly start to appreciate and even understand what's happening as a baby? A baby is helpless and even innocent from life itself. Back to miracles, back to phenomenon's, back to love, and devotion, too much to even say. But at some point, or at very early stages of this new and growing life. It becomes known or realized to the baby that they have this Angel, (this Momma,) and the dependency becomes a conscious state. Looking for Momma for food, nurturing, cleaning, learning, affection, and yes, the big one LOVE.

Amazing how this develops, not so much by instinct but also by some natural act of God. Yes, God is there from the blessed beginning and continues on and on. But Momma does all the work and always uncomplainingly with full and complete devotion. Devotion to what? Devotion to actually a " part" of her own self.

How can any type of a phenomenon be as or more profound? This "love", being, doing, grows exponentially, and is truly never ending. All of this love, devotion, breastfeeding, and diaper business seems endless. And at some point, early in this thing called life, this embryo, this fetus, this newborn, this child starts to understand there's a MOMMA. Certainly, a kind of love is to be known, a love that continues to be depending on and expecting of all this unquestionable "service", ongoing never ending and getting.

Momma is never without giving complete love. What an ideal position for baby. Baby who now starts to grow up. No more breast-feeding and not much more cuddling. Baby does grow up and the" baby" does not feel the dependency and strong need for their Momma. Just completely focused on themselves now, for their own selfish needs and wants, but now what about Momma? Where is Momma? She's gone, Momma did her job, exactly what was needed and expected of her. Now what? Offspring through natural stages of life grows up. Grows up to what? To another being maybe like Momma, maybe to get started in the same lifecycle.

Whatever prevails, still Momma should be remembered, to love, and now perhaps to be cared for. But that does not happen as naturally as all her servitude, and loving care. Where did it all go? Into the selfish, ungrateful, vain, egotistical minds, hands, and heart of our "baby". And Momma is no longer needed, no longer wanted in her separated place of "love". A new and different kind than from Momma's love. Sad and inconceivable that this happens and is the accepted "norm". Oh, she might get a Christmas card or even flowers on a birthday, perhaps even a visit on says Mother's Day? This is probably an act of conscience, or as maybe a thought of a " pay-back", but what comes around goes around. Poor Momma is on her own, hopefully able to care for herself, and perhaps even change her own diaper? But also, there is always the hopeful potential of the loving, caring, dedicated, devoted, beyond grateful, and appreciative Son or Daughter. They are there, there enough to make a difference. Perhaps to a chosen few. We must lower our expectations, because it does not always work in the way of Righteousness.

One Mother, just one Momma in this whole wide world. Where is she? So that I can embrace her, hold her close, kiss her, feel her warmth again. Her very breath, her being, her uncompromising LOVE. Bring her here, bring her back to me so I may tell her and have her just for that one moment again!

This being such a sensitive subject for me to be so presumptuous to write about. However, I understand not being a mother may restrict me somewhat. But having my own Mother, and experiencing my own immediate family life, particularly as a single parent Father, gives me some instinctive and loving concerns about Motherhood.

Father's Day

Narrative No. 28
June 10th, 2021

June 20th. Father's Day. National holiday on the calendar. Special Man, special Person. Webster had seven different definitions. We'll stay with the noun: "male parent." Not much glamour in that. The job does not call for glamour, just true love and uncompromising dedication. All by nature or instinct alone.

This goes deep, even to consider every type of living being. Go to the jungles, to the sea, to the mountains, to the prairies... Wherever. To the Zoo, to a nest, to a cave, to an alley. We can find a father, most always in attendance and care of his family.

Even think of the innocent penguin Father who carries the young, bodily in his care. Mom, yes, she's here to do most of the caring and all motherly duties. Usually dependent on Dad. But not all cases. That's part of what makes these thoughts interesting. The big factor of differences with Father and who he might be. This subject is infinite; however, we shall endeavor to explore our everyday life experiences and basic values for him.

A brilliant idea was derived not so very long ago. To have the father present and perhaps even assist in the actual delivery of his child. Yes, this is his very beginning moment of fatherhood. All in miracle fashion. The entire being and happening, each time in awe. However, first time Fathers in no way can start to imagine the true depth and outcome of this happening.

Mom and Dad can now put their lives on the back burner, it's all baby now, the only thing that is to matter. Well Dad can matter because he's about to earn it all. Earn it thru-out his lifetime. The man of the house, the protector, the provider. The one with the full responsibility to care and love all as one: as a family.

Now we leave the maternity facility as one, a new family. So, dad assumes all his duties and responsibilities gracefully, and naturally. Instinctively to know his part, right from day one and on and on. Being the provider is serious. Just to bear this full responsibility is awesome. But Dad moves on, working full time. Getting home and being a father is another full-time job.

Certainly, we know and fully acknowledge Mom, perhaps the true heroine. But look at Dad carrying the baggage for vacations, Helping with food shopping and much more. On the first day of college, there paying tuition, and on the side with maybe with a trunk on his back. Always there, working, shoveling snow, raking leaves, cutting lawn and hedges, cleaning up, cleaning gutters, painting, almost plumber, carpenter, electrician, whatever becomes necessary. Let's not forget. The diapers, the sleepless nights, even the baby sitting when called on. Quite a job, quite a career, quite a profession. Father, with Headaches and stress as a side bar.

But now he has his own National Holiday, deserving? You decide, when you are a father, to try to believe in your heart what you have accomplished. Perhaps on your day off, you can climb Mt. Everest? You are certainly prepared and perhaps bring the family along. They won't mind joining you. Happy Father's Day one and all.

Popi Plus

Narrative No. 29
August 19,2021

When it had been decided that I would become a grandfather it was not my decision, it was the Lords. Then at the age of 60, you might have said I was too old to handle it. Well for a while there, so did I, maybe for the brief moment of 4 to 5 minutes. But immediately after that fleeting period of adjustment, I came back down to earth. Suddenly to know what really happened. My daughter Diana had her first child, my first grandchild, My grandson. The most wonderful realization is to have a new addition to my own family. There I am into the new blessed beginning of one of the most wonders and exciting phases of my life.... it's truly amazing how life progresses.

You may now ask, where is my new babies' grandmother? She's looking "down "ready to help me on my new journey. Naturally with some added help from a few others.

The new Mommy with the new star soon to grow in our own constellation. Life does have its fair share of blessings, many yet to come. Wait.... this is just the beginning. Grandpa becomes an important player here. As much as God and his heart helps him,

How amazing this thing, sometimes so casually referred to as love, just becomes overwhelming. Why not? never forget that God is in charge, it can't get much better. Almost forgot to mention that my loving daughter Diana named my grandson Domenico after me.

This episode we have here now titled "Popi " is not exclusively mine. I graciously share it with all Popis. And again, to be accepted as a Holy Blessing to all, and baby too, and ready for his share. It's nowhere near possible to cover the full scenario with this brief commentary. Volumes have been written and infinitely more yet to be written (by others, thank you). We have our own family tree ready to share as the Lord will decide. All good.

So very much now to be done, new baby and all but not here, not now. This is a beginning into this new phase with Popi, the sometimes-silent partner. As a small part of our narratives on this humongous stage called life, Stay tuned for much more to be discovered. You say maybe this narrative does not belong in a book to interest the general public. But I know there are enough Parents and Grandparents out

there to have an interest in Popi's loving insight
into it all.

Offie

Narrative No. 30
May 23, 2020

It's a long road and sometimes a hard road. But we endure. It's love that makes it all possible. When you are with your loved ones everything feels so right. How precious it is to think now about these special times. My dear Offie leaves for home on Monday. She will be missed terribly. However, she will be home with her other part of her family, home in Peru. We shall share her. Although not to be here besides us she is surely in our hearts. That's the treasure.

A beautiful woman, mother, friend, my granddaughter's "Mother-in- law". As for me, a "friend" is not enough to say. Her presence is so warm, so loving you feel her every ounce. Never without a smile, Her laughter right along. She has stolen all our hearts. Hardly ever to realize what precious moments mean as you are living them. But with Offie gone you do realize how precious she really is. What a blessing to have her, although far apart. She will be back soon, that comforts us a little, maybe a little more than a little.

We are selfish at times without meaning to be. Not fair to want to keep Offie for ourselves, but she is ours. Being apart from loved ones is very hard, but just the thought of her is a warm feeling that helps you endure. We still have her right here always in our hearts. That's part of life, accepting this kind of longing. We know for sure that we will be together again, such a happy exciting thought for us.

Let's think about Offie's feelings too. We know how much she misses us and how her thoughts are about us. Loving and missing and wanting to be near us. But time passes swiftly and the very thought of being together again is the greatest comfort. Just knowing of the times already spent here together is comforting. Comforting to remember the nearness and the fun with the loving togetherness. That is our reward and there will be a lot more to come. Feeling better already. That's what Offie does to you. She makes you feel a lot better just by the very thought of her. A very special kind of person. God gave us Offie to love. She is family, and family is the very foundation of life.

Near or afar we are always together in our minds and especially in our hearts. We know Offie misses us as much as we miss her. But she is here with us even when we're apart. That's the thoughts to have and never to doubt. We're a loving family and certainly Offie is an important part. How fortunate and such a blessing to carry these thoughts and feelings within ourselves. That's all part of living and accepting the good with the bad.

475 words about our dear Offie . How easy, how sad, how happy, how glad. To have her near always then to have her back almost like she never was gone. But she was gone, and we missed her, and she missed us. But now back, such happy, happy thoughts. That's the best way to feel to make it through.

544 words, still not enough, but will have to do for now, at least until February of 2022. Not so bad, not so far, not too fret.

Now up to 573 we can keep going without even trying but by the time this story ends, here she is, Back! ......Feels Good...... 596.... that's a wrap!

My Buddy

Narrative No. 31
August 18, 2021

"Friend": noun: A person one knows well and likes. Mr. Webster helps me get started. This is about friends and friendship. Also, to acknowledge "friendly" as the adjective: as kindly and helpful. We can know right there what this all means. Very clear and very natural. When you are fortunate to have a friend, you are then very fortunate. Also, he is to be as an ally. I have had many friends all of which I felt privileged to be with. This relationship can be casual and natural. That is the basic spirit of it all. The ease of your togetherness. A special relationship. Always as low keyed.

Most always friends have a lot in common. Which attracts and builds upon (usually a close age bracket). There are several categories which I shall expand on. Start with "casual". This may be a job associate, which is kind of restrained but worthy. Working together does require an intimacy of some kind. Really to function in harmony and basically to respect each other's partnership. This is comfortable and should be so for seven hours a day. Keep it relaxed and natural. A nice category that can spill over and extend beyond casual. This is the best part of friendship, there are no hard rules or even guidelines, that's how a friendship functions.

Next to move on to another category, "a social pal". Maybe even as your golfing buddy. Good comfortable arrangement. Friendship is not to be confused with family. Such as a great brother-in-law, favorite uncle or close cousin or even your Siamese twin. Friendship is basically outside of family. All as respecting with no obligations of any kind. The social pal friendship is rewarding as it is pleasurable, to enjoy fun events such as a ball game or a car show. All worthwhile.

Now to move into our final category: "Your best friend". This is the intent of this narrative. The other categories just served to emphasize the true meaning of Friendship. Putting Mr. Webster aside. Now we're getting into "Blood Brothers", metaphorically of course. You can be in the same room together, not even to speak, but still to communicate. Your Buddy, seven feet tall, always "there". How fortunate for me to have experienced such bonding. A salient part of my life that forms all into the shape of a friend. One of many factors is, this is the person that can almost share it with your mother or your wife (but not quite). He's here now with us, in spirit and in heart, this is as deep as it gets, short of tears. He's not your 24/7 army pal. That was wartime, but he's close in a different way.

We shared a 35-year friendship up to his sudden demise 10 years ago and I miss him badly. Grieving can have a good side to it. The part of remembering all those precious memories along with the serious moments. Some things may have been forgotten but not much. Whatever may have been forgotten, still was lived and shared all as precious times. This living part with all the memories, can be saddening in ways at times. It is for us to realize the treasures we still have and what we did have. It is difficult to accept and learn to live with the absence however with no options. "Friend " is a warm word to speak and moving to do so. I have written several narratives skimming this subject of "friendship" always preoccupied with "family" which is in a class of its own. It's a marvel how the mind can behave, coupled with the heart when you do get into very sensitive matters, particularly parts of the past which are all gone. This writing now is something of a comfort. All these words, all these feelings I carry with me every day. You must keep the treasures in your heart, your heart certainly has a big job to do. Read my scenario (Narrative No.52) On Two Separate Hearts all in one body. Somewhat as a fantasy but not meant to be. Here I am just reaching out to share, I know I'm not alone in grieving and I take advantage of this "book" opportunity. To perhaps lend comfort to a few. I deal with true feelings. That's the benchmark for most of my stories.

But true friendship is solid gold, requiring no effort just as natural as breathing. It does sadden me to reminisce in this way, but it warms me to remember that I had such a friend as a partner. Knowing and sharing the same feelings and beliefs as one. I keep exploring the depth of this kind of friendship and revel in the memory of having been together. No pretense between us ever, just that special understanding. What a comfort of thought to have had such a friend that has always been unconditionally there for you as you have been for him. It's lonely without my buddy: Cesare A. Tacrmina. I just keep his memory alive. After all, "What Are Friends For"?

A Christmas Story

Narrative No. 32
December 31, 2019

On New Year's Eve, while on the phone with my daughter Diana, sitting on my couch in my living room, opposite my trees. My two Christmas trees were right opposite, within reach. I focused on the light decorations of different colors: Red, Blue, Green, Yellow, with a White light at the top near the Star. At this moment I thought of all my Dearly Departed loved ones and friends, each as a different light and knowing they will always be in our hearts, Christmas time and throughout the year. Let the blinking ones speak and be so dear with all thought of as their own beings and sharing our love with them all.

We love them, miss them and pray for them all always and keep them warm in our hearts, as present, with precious and happy thoughts. Our Christmas tree is the ultimate knowing of always being together. As seen and felt near with each light. Some blinking, as a greeting. And let us always refer to our loved ones in the present tense knowing as to their always being here and never in the past tense, as to being away and gone, present now as we feel at Christmas Time and always.

It's a heavy heart and always will be. A moment away from a tear but always remembering our treasure and the comfort to feel how strong love and endearment can be with every thought, breath and heartbeat. Not easy but still our only comfort.

This is the very first of my narratives, the one that motivated all the others and my book. Read the sequel No. 33.

A Christmas Story Sequel

Narrative No. 33
February 16, 2019

The days have passed but the season has not
ended
The tree lights are off, and the tree is down
Christmas is not solely one day
The spirit will always stay
The lights that shone so bright that last night
Will never go off in our hearts and sight
All those precious memories and thoughts
Stay with us always in prayer and in sorts
Our loved ones are truly missed in this present
life
We embrace them with love through sorrow and
strife
Keep their lights burning and never forget
How fortunate life was that we all met
It seems somehow strange
That all that remains
Is the star from the top.
So, look up at the Heavens and see all those
stars.
And never forget that's where they all are.
Keep the memories alive, along with their
smiles.

Hear their voices, see their faces across the
miles
See all the faces smiling so bright
Keep their lights burning throughout your whole
life
Our heart-warming lights, they all burn so bright
The spirits remain each day of your life.
Each moment into days will always be alive
Keep your heart warm and with all of them
inside
I miss my tree already. But don't measure your
own life
In years, months or days and lonely nights.
Think of it all with songs and smiles
The love will be there in spite of the miles.
They look down every day and missing you as
well
Knowing that someday your bell will knell.

I'm Talking Here

Narrative No. 34
May 10, 2021

Most of what I do or say I believe is not completely understood. Not to say I'm above the "fray" it just seems I may be going too fast for some. I know it immediately when I pass them right by. At this very moment I certainly know that I am endowed as blessed with a holy spirit. So, what to do? Absolutely nada. Just hang on and enjoy the ride. A very special, fun kind of experience. I feel invincible, clever, confident, proud and more. Just here and now to share it all. Strange and mysterious as may be. Like I know it all, far be it, but faith does offer a certain degree of confidence and somewhat "power". Power to do good for all those in need. So be it. I see beauty everywhere.

Hear Me Now

Narrative No. 35
June 24, 2021

Let it be known now. This writing being indicative as a "Prayer", shall be understood to be as my own humble request to my own God. Not intended or to be construed as a religious doctrine. And to make no presumptions otherwise.

I found this prayer hiding in my heart. And although this has been said in many ways before, I find it now time to share with all. Simply as: "Hear Me Now". Our Dear and Holy Father in Heaven Above. We send this prayer to you, telling of our love and devotion. Within the spirit of thine own love for all, we beseech thee to look over us with your care and goodness, receive our love with understanding and forgiveness, allowing us to remain safe in your heart forever. Amen.

Your Golden Cross

Narrative No. 36
March 15, 2020

He's here with you for all to see
Around your neck and near your heart
Your prayers are heard, this will always be
Be sure never to part
The true power of faith and prayer
We believe will always be there
Now open your eyes and see where you are
Right here with me always from here to a star.
Push away all demons and make it be known
That in your heart you will never be alone
So, hold this cross and never forget
It's meaning and know that we met.
God is your fountain to drink, and you will never
thirst
Just always remember to keep Him first.
Your Golden Cross, all shining and bright
To guide you and keep you in God's loving light.
So, keep this cross ALWAYS and always to
know
Of our love truly, which never will go.
So, keep this cross ALWAYS and always to say
'I'm right here beside you, and always to stay'.

Mind You

Narrative No. 37
October 22, 2021

The heart being basically a pump for your blood circulation and other body functions, also as being a muscle, a partial distinction between the human mind and the heart. I tend to believe the mind dominates and has control over the heart, The mind has no limits, always in complete charge.

Always endeavor to keep a strong will so you may exercise a certain avenue of control, allowing you to personally govern your own actions with mind and thoughts. Such an interesting study you can make to consider how you can try to perform to your desired best interest. Mind over matter, Infinite considerations can be made. Even trying to reason the mind's functioning with this mild narrative analysis here and now. This review is only as a casual curiosity not pretending to be from a medical source or journal. We must strive to maintain control of our thoughts and actions with the use of our mind and our own sincere intentions. Keep a healthy mind and in turn allow for a healthy and stable life.

Late Again?

Narrative No. 38
November 7, 2021

She felt that constant feeling of eyes on her even in bed sleeping, a kind of sensation like someone was there right in her bedroom. This was not possible as she had a very sophisticated alarm system along with sensors in her small apartment in Greenwich Village, Manhattan, on Jane Street. This alarm system was the results of the strange happenings at home and strange noises during the night in the wee hours. She would be awakened by the shower running (scary), then to get up to turn it off and sense a presence. Without any sign or indication of disturbance or intrusion on any part of the alarm system and now with a strange and mysterious odor in the room. She felt not alone making the effort to get back to sleep but was unable. Just lying-in bed half-awake but frightened and now with the alarm clock going off she jumped and started her workday as usual, showering and dressing and then ready for a quick breakfast. Much to her surprise the kitchen was warm with the smell of toast and the table was set for two. In a very frightened state, she dashed out of her place locking the double lock behind. She had her car in the building garage which she only used on the weekends basically to visit family in Connecticut. For work she used public transportation, NYC Subway System off at South Ferry last stop and down the block to Chamber Street. The workday was always pleasant; however, she constantly had the feeling of being watched. A definite sensation.

Her workstation was uncomfortable today. A feeling like it had been disturbed and even searched. She did report it to security and the office surveillance tapes did indicate some activity with strange shadows in her work area all in the wee hours of the morning. Also, she reported once again that familiar odor now at her workstation. A quiet workday then the subway home for a peaceful evening.

She hardly slept. She had an uneasy feeling again of a presence in the apartment almost beside her. And yet she overslept from sheer anxiety, and strangely the alarm failed to go off. Showering and dressing quickly she dashed out with no breakfast, just a heavy anxiety knowing her office had strict hours and did not tolerate tardiness under any accounts. Frantically she rode a taxi to work and now with a slight feeling of relief believing she'd make it by minutes.to spare. However, upon entering the office everyone was busy at their workstations, the place was buzzing. With her obvious late arrival, a sudden silence came over the entire room.

She was exactly one hour late. Not possible but she was seeing the clock in the entry, yes one hour, 60 minutes late. There was her supervisor sitting working at her station. After an embarrassing public reprimand, she settled down to work and surprisingly found a rose on her desk, fresh as can be. Upon starting with her laptop ready for work the sudden shock to realize her entire work material content on her laptop was gone, everything completely deleted, erased. A near impossible scramble to make a semblance of a workday. All in a state of complete confusion and anxiety; then finally the end of a long hard day.

She left wearily for home. Stopping off in the local market for a prepared meal although completely without an appetite. At last safe at home. Only to have that same feeling as having been watched all the way home and now once more that feeling of a presence, again with the strange odor. The table had been set again for two, all a bewilderment. Now to suddenly realize that all the clocks in the apartment were set back, one hour. This was truly frightening just to know someone had been here. Here in the privacy of her home. Table was set and all. She immediately called the superintendent on her cell phone. Inquiring about this entire happening and of any sign of any strange activity particularly in or around her apartment. Nothing unusual happened today, nothing reported. The Supt.appearing to have strong doubts about the entire complaint. Another sleepless night unable to relax at all.

Still that same sensation of another presence in the apt. After awakening an extra hour early and racing again with taxi, and no breakfast. Now at work racing up the stairs, not to wait for an elevator she arrived early at a dark empty office with the cleaning person advising her it was Saturday with the office obviously closed. Sitting at her dark station she was completely overwhelmed by all these bizarre happenings. Looking now to just race home and lock the door and jump into bed.

Race home she did. It was getting dark with an overcast and the start of rain. And she did notice a shadow in the closed storefront below her apartment building. Again, sensing that strange familiar odor. Following a quick reaction, she snapped a photo with her cell. The shadow seemed startled. Then she ran into her building and up the stairs quickly.

Home at last securing the double locks. The same familiar odor and the same feeling as someone had been here in her very apartment. Looking around only to see her closet rummaged with clothing scattered and dresses on the floor. Racing once again down to the Supt's apt. He now reacted as very annoyed with the interruption. She insisted on the locks being changed. He assured her it will be done Monday morning.

With great hesitation she re-entered her own apartment in fear. Not able to have the appetite to eat, she cleaned up the closet, got into pajamas and almost in bed when she remembered to set her alarm, setting two reliable electric alarm clocks forgetting the next day was Sunday, the only chance to sleep if. When the alarms did go off early, she jumped in the shower and dressed, suddenly realizing it was Sunday. Very upset with herself but consoled by the reliability of her two alarms. Spent the best part of the day restoring her laptop and resetting her clothes closet. Well early to bed after a quick-frozen dinner figuring to awaken extra early on Monday morning Now setting both alarms at least a half hour ahead of her normal wake-up time. Both alarms are set early, not to worry. Ready for that cranky supervisor at work. And then to come home to new locks. Things were starting to feel better and almost back to normal. Lights out now and, bring on that Monday, she was ready.

She awakened frantically wondering why the two alarms did not go off yet. Here she was on the brink of being late again. Only now to realize the power failure on this rainy blue Monday. In her now cold apartment with the power outage affecting the heating system. Assuring herself she had the time to shower, which sounded good for a fresh start. There she was in a cold shower with no hot water. The outage again. Now back in the same race to get to work on time. Really wound up. No breakfast, no heat, cold shower and maybe late again. Taxi as her best hope. Not so good, rainy Monday mornings in Manhattan, traffic worse than ever. Knowing it was getting late and within a few blocks of the office, deciding she can walk faster than the traffic. Now in the torrential rain on Chamber Street. We know the clock keeps ticking and now for sure she's' late again and she forgot her laptop at home with all her updated work programs. Taking the stairs once more, again to minimize her lateness. And there he was "Mr. Nice Guy" sitting at her desk, (without the rose), obviously fuming: Enter the Very Late, The Very Exhausted Poor Soul, Like A Wet Sponge……..

Big scene…. Big Confrontation, all office activities came to a halt, what else could go wrong.? She was fired…. finished. Where did it all start? And where and when will it end.? She managed to drag her wet self-home only to find new locks and a crowd in her apartment. Two policemen with the Supt. And some strange looking creature and with that strange familiar odor, wearing her best dress. Now to find out she has been evicted…. Out… with no job and now with no home minus her best dress. Furniture and all in storage, car packed, now back to Mom and Dad in Connecticut. Only to find out later from a former neighbor that this was all a plot to get her out by the Supt to find this precious village apartment for his brother/sister? In her best dress, no less

Heartache

Narrative No. 39
June 12th, 2021

A message to a certain someone:
Sure, it hurts, and it'll hurt for a long time. But it's not fair to you to have this heavy heart. The old saying goes: So, you missed that trolley car but don't fret, another one will come along," and it always does. I know it can be lonely waiting for the next trolley car, but just think when it does come, how happy and joyful you'll be. Everything will be so special you won't even think of the old heart aches. So easy to say, so easy to write, but it's all part of living. There's no escaping it. Be strong and have confidence. Confidence in yourself and in your faith
You are entitled like everyone else to grieve. When the better times come, you'll know it. It's wonderful to be happy, a feeling all of its own. But appreciate your good times, your happy times. This makes everything feel worthwhile. The hard work, the worrying, the stress, the sacrifices, the lonely times. All part of what we must endure. And for sure, you will not

be overlooked. Each and every day is precious and important for you to appreciate.

Let's not waste a single one. Sure, you look around and you wonder just to see all those happy people. Where is my share? Where is my happiness? You may be happy right now, in this moment and not even know it. Sure, that sounds silly. Life is one long hard road, different and not the same for everyone. Some find happiness and contentment earlier than others and some find it in many different ways. Your happiness is coming. It's not for you to dwell on a broken heart, pick up the option, to be happy. This world is your Oyster, scoop it up. And that is to move on, be your own best friend, and find your rainbow, it's there.

Mr. Webster

For me, my Dictionary is a necessary tool for my writing, and reading. Mr. Webster is a reliable reference, basically for definitions. However other features are worthy, such as: Pronunciation, Speech Labels (i, e, noun, adjective, etc.), Helpful illustrations, and much more. Also, the Etymology or word history defined by Mr Webster as "The origin and development of a word".

How interesting to find a disclaimer, there for limits of liability. It never occurred to me as to the exposure for legal liability as a simple dictionary. We must accept this as part of todays' "norm".

It would be interesting to research the origin and development of the dictionary itself. (Just a curious thought), so proper and complete in all its ways. Basic evaluation as commonly used for a definition. Certainly, for me, more.

I am always concerned about verifying correct spelling and for reference as guidance for better usage of a word. On rare occasions I might not find a word I seek. Which may lead me to doubt as its actual existence. I am dependent upon Mr., Webster. (Maybe even intellects use dictionaries) to occasionally browse and gather up a new word or two.

My narrative here was my intent to present Mr. Webster as a friend. Brought on to help me write and define my stories whether as stories, essays, compositions, poems, prose or such, but finally decided on as" my narratives".

Mr. Websters can be found in my car, bedroom and also comfortable on my kitchen table, within my reach. Always available for ready reference and I feel most confident with his nearness.

Here I am glorifying our everyday dictionary. Why not make this opportunity to celebrate him? Perhaps if only as a literary exercise and be challenged to find a duller subject. Also try to attract interest. with an endeavor for: Colloquial Dialogue.

Next time you pick up a dictionary, don't look for me, just think of me. Check under "D" just in case Mr. W decides to reciprocate. Having fun here satisfying a mental challenge.

My Romance

Narrative No. 41
July 7th, 2021

Today was a good day, with full anticipation for a strong and relatively active day. Having been fully rested to a maximum. Sad to say, a strong day for me is truly not an extraordinary day but average. All daily activities engaged as essential, to include my music never as a burden, really more like a love.

My expectations with my musical studies are limited. However, I am capable of playing my guitar overcoming minor handicaps. Exercising my hands with silly putty is most effective and beneficial. However, playing becomes completely dependent upon hand and finger dexterity. I am reasonably satisfied with my playing as progressively improving.

It is a fact that my quest for learning to play guitar is not only dependent upon physical dexterity but also focus. Favoring music that I know reduces the challenge. I am not blessed with either talent or being gifted, however with a strong will and determination. To me "to thine own self be true". I know my limitations, A matter of strong will and want. I'm starting my seventh consecutive year of formal study with a qualified instructor.

Basically, I keep this whole scenario as casual because I never want this learning quest to become a burden or a frustration. I have several guitars in my apartment, almost one in every room. What a convenience and what an incentive.

Later in a separate narrative, I'll make a light comparison to my early days of playing the saxophone, an interesting and curious reason to define the profound distinction between a string instrument and a wind instrument. Let's say with the strings, I feel a more personal and intimate relationship with my guitar. I will later comment on my newly found love with my ukulele. Another story. But today was exhilarating for me, music wise.

I am reaping the reward for organizing my music, sheets and books. This has improved my practice, playing into a more casual, productive program. My repertoire today consists of many songs, all very selectively chosen. Old standard ballads of which I am most familiar with. Just songs from way back.

With this new organizing of my music. Now my practice session flows with ease and fun, my kind of fun.

Being a virtuoso is not my intent, however some days are better than others. All I'm trying to make known here and now is my interest and intimate relationship with my guitar. "My romance," I get a feeling of pride and satisfaction from my music. Not with any specific goals or plans, just the flow of it all to know that I can enjoy that part of my day. A special way to escape with reward. I don't expect to ever reach a level to perform, just a simple stage of entertaining myself. Today being quite a good day, as music lightens my overall day. I am completely free to play whenever I feel like it, wee hours of the morning included.

Something about the sound of strings that's so pleasant and peaceful, just to be able to play my favorites, good days feel good. It's encouraging to approach any level of improvement or betterment. I am not in competition with myself, only enjoying this wonderful advantage and opportunity for "My Romance".

My Box with Six Strings

Narrative No. 42
September 5, 2021

This book is basically composed of short stories made up of various subject matter and scenarios. I now get to the soul: Music/Guitar. My personnel pandemic. I'm hooked and have been most of my adult life.

My musical studies started with the saxophone, a brass wind instrument. Followed now by "My Box with Strings".... The guitar. Love at first sight. I don't know how this fascination escaped me for so long. Perhaps there are certain times in life for everything.

Well, I started with an inexpensive guitar as a factor of finances. Another factor being 50 cent lessons from "Charlie" the local barber. Lacking the enthusiasm then, it became an intermittent study on and off through the years, however that box with strings captivated me in a serious way, about 10 years ago. Brought on by I know not what. Perhaps a simple Six Tuesday night adult course.

The instrument became meaningful to me, and I ultimately started to take serious lessons with a more qualified instructor and a much better guitar. Studying a musical instrument is strongly dependent upon a certain degree of musical aptitude, relating to a certain innate talent. A heavy call. Some people are naturals, some are even gifted. However, I was neither, but I loved it.

Having the desire to learn became absolutely overwhelming. Learning naturally puts a demand on practicing. But the desire and the devotion shines through. You must want it, not necessarily in some fanatical manner, but "to want" is the key. My contentions and desire to learn is what I want. I enjoy playing guitar. As a pastime for relaxation fun and for even "escape", this is my answer.

Not solely entertaining any false modesty. I truly realize my limitations, but I have dedication, because It's enjoyable and somewhat rewarding. However, I feel as if I have "peaked" in my learning and playing ability. This narrative was more intended to focus on the instrument more than my playing ability, but the union is intimate.

I presently have a guitar in every room with the exception of the laundry and bathroom. However, a strong contender would be my ukulele to peek in. It's gratifying just to joke about it. A string instrument to me is a more intimate type of musical instrument.

Merely just the manner of having to hold and almost embrace it, serves as part of the bond. Strings have a softness to be a blending of the music that I favor, all from the almost forgotten era of big bands with legendary musicians and vocalists.

As an honorable mention in the category of "Greats" brings me to tell of my brief friendship with the great Bucky Pizzarelli. A fine man, as well as a great guitarist. Bucky was part of a historical period in American music. with" Big Bands" the likes of which may never be seen again; Glen Miller, Benny Goodman, Tommy and Jimmy Dorsey, Paul Whiteman, Vaughn Monroe, Harry James, Stan Kenton, Gene Krupa, and many others.

Bucky as being a part of this historical music era. And that music is classical even to this day. Many are aware of this period. My digressing is inevitable with the guitar being a prevalent part of it all. That's the music that I favor with my guitar.

"My Box with Strings" is an important part of my life right now. My love for the instrument is to an extreme. To hear the mellow sound of the strings is my reward along with my eagerness to progress with the quality of my playing. But this "Box". is fascinating. A marvel in its structure to create the sounds is a wonder to me. I long for each moment to just pick one up and to hold it. Even the basics of tuning, as a nurturing. It is essential for the guitar to always be in correct tune, making for the sound desired as well as the correctness as necessary, allowing for the true pleasure of playing.

Duets are fun and also rewarding. Somewhat challenging to be in sync with the music as with each other. And a major reward is to vocalize along.

Just to have a side interest as a student and as a hobby, is a happy and kind of productive pastime. A fun and a relaxing way to spend leisure time and for professionals. A livelihood.

I shall continue with my pursuit to play better and enjoy each session. Mr. Webster defines the guitar as "A musical instrument with usually 6 strings, plucked with the fingers or a plectrum (or pic)". As a footnote Bucky played his 7-string signature guitar. I prefer to call my Yamaha, named "Harmony", my friend. You may now want to put my book back on the shelf and run out and buy a guitar.........Preferably a six string......

Music, Music

Narrative No. 43
July 16, 2021

Today, Friday July 16th, was very exciting for me. A video was made right before me. Exciting? Not yet. Hang on. About a month ago a little tune kept spinning around in my head. Me as a student of guitar can almost expect that, not really something new and original. I pecked away the notes on my guitar, liking it more each time. Just a few notes then off to the side. Then a few days later this tune captivated me so much that I composed the words to a song. Actually, the melody was suggestive for my lyrics. I tried to compose the melody along with the words. That was not happening. Trying with the help of my guitar it started to progress. Just a little. Now the natural thing to do is to write it out, however, not so easy, the words yes but not the actual notes. Mind you this is all coming from a beginner/beginner guitar student. I will report on my previous study with the saxophone seventy-three years ago. Playing sax for a few years up to when Uncle Sam beckoned, then off I went into the military. Now we're drifting far from my original video story. But we will catch up, promise. The actual writing of the notes I find difficult, notwithstanding my ability to read music. Simply not the same. However, I did manage to Write a few lines of actual notes. All suggestive of my words, which was my driving force. This is sounding like a "Moon Shot". Hardly, L simply Contributed to composing a little song. But what a thrill for me when my collaborator Frank put my words to music. Frank Rudolph being a very accomplished musician and my guitar instructor. He made the "video" performing with the vocals and guitar very nicely professionally as well. So, my little persistent tune buzzing became a nice new country/western tune. How happy and proud I am. This is Willie and Dolly all the way. Must copyright: "How Can I Be Without You".

Next adventure, maybe climb Mt. Everest with my guitar. It might be easier?

Ukes Are Cute

Narrative No. 44
January 13, 2021

All I want to do is play my uke
The sound makes me happy
The touch makes me play

When I hold her, she fits so right to stay
Only four strings to play
So many songs to sing
All I want to do is play my uke
That's all the fun she brings
Morning noon and night
It always feels so right

We are so cozy together
Like birds of a feather
My fingers are so tender
Just make me surrender

To my little friend
There is no end

My guitar is the star
And the uke is the nuke

All I hear are happy sounds
Every time a tune goes around
And every note is a song of its own
Like something I've never known

Twenty-four hours is not enough.
To keep up with all this stuff.

G. C. E. A.
"Good Cats Eat Apples"

Narrative No. 45
March 29, 2021

       G.C.E.A. The Four Strings on The Uke. Right to the very core, and then, they want some more. This guide helps me tune my strings and keeps my songs so bright. It's only too bad that I start my music so late at night. So, what does it matter? The feelings are still the same, and I'm so glad I came.

       On to music with such sheer delight. Something very special in my life. I could be better, but whatever. I still have fun with everyone and by the ton, when I play my guitar. My ukulele is different, it's like a "Soprano" in "C". But I find it to be like a newborn infant in my arms, and to be sure that no harm will come, with my playing a bit, the strap I use, so I'll never lose my hold on it. This instrument is "happy", it's so easy to hear. Maybe that's why I hold it so dear.

       Back to the G.C.E.A. This signifies the four strings in order on a uke. I named my Uke Jude. But my guitar is my best friend, the uke is a close runner up. However, I've been struggling with music studies for almost seven years. I am now at the point of perhaps playing reasonably well (who's to say). Despite my extenuating arthritis, failing eyesight, fried mind, and defective vocal cords. But I think the true spirit of music is not to demand perfection. However, skill and accomplishment help. Gifted is certainly appreciated as the pinnacle.

I have my own values here. Music is an escape and provides diversion and relief, relief from everyday stress. Music is fun, all those ingredients are the bases for my motivation and interest. So, I will continue enjoying it, however I do, and if someone happens to enjoy it, that's wonderful too! On to the glockenspiel and harmonica.

BUCKY

Narrative No. 46
August 25, 2021

Bucky Pizzarelli the world renown jazz guitarist musician. I met him for the first time in the Lyceum Theatre in the roundabout 20 years ago, about 2001. Performing as a trio, he played lead with a Benedetto 7 String guitar. Frank Vinola, back up with a fellow on stand-up base. Great show to a full house. I was in awe just to be in the same room with him. A living legend.

This was a theatre in the round in Sugar loaf N.Y. I had great seats about 15 feet away from Bucky. Frank and base were right on. Their playing respect for Bucky was what it should have been. Bucky played in his own style of greatness. Most of the old standards: Gershwin, Duke, Rogers and Hart, Berlin, Mercer, Porter, Kern and on. And I then met Bucky for the first time. He was about 75 at that time and played in his usual style of greatness. This was an exciting experience for me. Knowing of Bucky's background was enough to be in awe. Then to see him perform was beyond my wildest dream. I believe his guitar playing beginning may have been as a youngster about 10 years of age, with an uncle as his teacher. As a teenager Bucky started sitting in with top pros. At that time music was more casual and greatly improvised particularly Jazz.

Bucky was in the right place at the right time. So much talent around then. The age of big bands: Artie Shaw, Tommy and Jimmy Dorsey, Paul Whiteman, Harry James, Glen Miller, with Bunny Berrigan, Bix Biederbeck, Duke Ellington, Kruper, Basie, Nat Cole, Fats Waller, Ella Fitzgerald, Rosemary Clooney, Sinatra, Jack Teagarden, Tony Matola, Al Caiola, Les Paul, Stan Getz, on and on.

The music industry was booming along with all that great talent and Bucky along with them His career blossomed early. He was a natural for the times. The guitar also was fitting for the times. The guitar was also popular for back-up and accompaniment for lead vocalists. Most of his early beginning was before T.V., All live shows, local vaudeville, and lots of road work. Radio was big at the time for music.

I believe Bucky did a tour of duty in the U. S. Army at the close of W.W. 2. Now with a very successful career and enjoying a good family life in New Jersey. Along with his wife Ruth, sons Martin and John, and two daughters, one Mary and another unknown to me. All children with an association with music. Son

John, on to great fame and success, an int'l star.

All family loving Bucky continued to perform publicly almost to the end. I have attended many of his live performances, mostly at the landmark Ritz Theatre in Newburgh N.Y. And developed a casual friendship with some photos. I will always think of Bucky as a friendly, kind, loving man with charisma beyond just music and guitar. He created the extra string, with the seven-string guitar, his signature guitar with seven strings also as his license plate on his Mercedes SUV and as a thought here, Bucky being an active artist as well. I viewed a showing of his artwork in the Ritz theatre.

My casual and intermittent interest and study with guitar started in 1957. 64 years ago. Bucky was my earliest inspiration.

Guitar study allows for the respect, pleasure, and appreciation for the skill, talent and dedication. All as required to gain from the desire and effort to play with any degree of satisfaction and reward along with some pride. Bucky has performed with some of the greatest names in 'show business' history, some as mentioned above with his name ranking as great among them. This all now as my Tribute

with my highest regard, to my Friend Bucky
Pizzarelli with his revered memory.:1925-2020.

Django

Narrative No. 47
June 15th, 2021

DJANGO......... A great gypsy guitarist from the past. Try to catch your breath. This is what heaven must be like with his sound. His "New York" gig video is grueling, dueling. Catch each solo, just beautifully incredible. Some can never even start to imagine what can be done with music, and the guitar. Far, far into the beyond.

If you have any interest at all in music and the guitar in particular. Just two words for you. Only two: Django Reinhardt. That's it!

Never can you believe what you're hearing is truly happening. The incredibility of it all is a phenomenon. How is this humanly possible? Are there no limits to his mind and talent? Just to witness and hear such a happening as an experience that cannot be expressed or communicated other than by Mr. Django. Imagine you being his guitar being brought to such heights, unimaginable. Is this reality? Such an epitome, such a world to be in. Anyone who has ever picked up a guitar, can simply be transfixed and mesmerized.

This playing skill cannot be believed. It is a marvel to even realize what is happening when Django is on. Beyond just "playing" this is a category that may not even exist, but it did. Is "it" with us today? Nowhere even near hardly. Dgango Reinhardt: 1910-1953. Yes, he was here and yes, he did it all. I can only hope that people have the opportunity to hear it and grasp it. Music aficionado or not, you have had to be moved by this experience with Dgango. Not even to say: once in a lifetime, never that fortunate. Perhaps a special kind of reward to be thankful for. Only 315 words, nowhere near enough for him. Just listen to him, words are not necessary, only reverence with the feeling of deep emotion and awe.

Stay Don't Go

Narrative No 48
August 1, 2021

This is the making of a song, I want to share: (Country Western style)

"Where do we go from here? You hardly shed a tear. It's like you saw it coming, and I was so at ease. Everything as you please. So, I guess it had to happen, you with your finger snapping at every guy in the room, I should have sensed the doom. What we do right now. will tell us both somehow, about what it all meant from the start. I guess I never really had your heart. We may go our separate ways but who's to really say that's the right thing to do, because I'll go on loving you.
I'll miss you for sure there's no other cure but for you to stay you also know it's so. Let's make up right now we both know how. Come into my arms and succumb to my charms. We are meant to be, anyone can see. Let's make it last forever., With our strong endeavor, we still have that chance to patch up our romance.

Stay and we both will gain and avoid any more pain. I can see in your eyes not to sever our ties. I feel better to have you back with me. Stay at my side and be my bride. Make our whole loving future together and have one another to live to enjoy a life that will grow with family and love and strife, and to look back to know that you made it so." Stay Please Don't Go".

Always

Narrative No. 49
July 24th, 2021

The guitar is my means of expression. Certainly not intended as a private means. Although practicing mostly alone becomes private. Playing songs, I truly like, mostly my favorites. Most of which are long gone and even obsolete. The oldies bring back olde tymes and memories. Pity I lost my voice and lost the fun part. Maybe that's what exaggerates the sweetness of these old songs. But I know it's just the righteousness of the melody and the lyrics. Some above others, such as an old Irving Berlin song, written in 1924. The song is titled: "Always". I get teary eyed each time it's heard. In fact, even more when I play it.

"Always "has the tender lyrics that say it all. Strongly to bring back very precious memories. This was the song at my Mother and Father's wedding on June 26, 1926. Also played at my wedding to my Wife Ginny on Sept. 1st. 1956, thirty years later. And with the same musician, Raymond Rizzone, my father's first cousin on violin.

Here I am now, 91 and 65 years later, reminiscing what this song means to me. The lyrics are simple and so beautiful. Starting with: "I'll be loving you always". Just so tender. Dolly Parton said it a little differently, as: "I Will Always Love You ". All the same in my heart. All The words and music are so right. But now to remember and re-live is sad and happy at the same time.

The thought here is this power of a song. Just imagine my gratification to play memorable songs like this on my guitar. What a treasure chest. Me with my guitar and my music, an awful lot to feel and to share, But all so natural. What a reward for me to enjoy this to the fullest.

Sometimes you choose to hide from loss and sadness, because it hurts so, but the ability to reminisce a loved one is somewhat comforting. Music, as an escape from reality. However, reality is real, with truly no escape.

Keep a strong mind always with the effort to live with major misfortunes and losses. Really misfortunes coupled with all as part of this thing called life. Don't even think of future sorrows, it's not a fair way to live. Do your best not to dwell on sadness and enjoy all that you now have. Enjoy and appreciate thoughts of good times here and to come. Now back to my guitar to stay lighthearted and to resume my sentiments like "Always". Imagine 436 words to comfort your heart with love, Always....

Previously Owned, Pure Fiction

"Elwis ", my favorite guitar. All scarred, defaced and violated. Let's try to imagine his journey here, to me. The imagination is salted with some facts. Facts: like we know his Model No. Yamaha F 315 A, Made in Indonesia. Serial No. 30725057 Hard to guess his age. First a reference to the serial number then it might be worthwhile to substantiate the date of model discontinuance. A likely guess about 15 to 20 years old. I can imagine the first owner enjoying him. And him leading a normal life of a guitar. Maybe a second sale to a young student, again Elwis with a normal existence. Just guessing all the way. Maybe some isolated closet time. Maybe another sale turn-over.

Getting close to a period of gloom along with a" perpetrator, "who I will guess being some Rock freak about 30. Probably on drugs. Able to play somewhat. Nowhere near accomplished. Poor Elwis just making it. Probably with old strings, which have consequences here. The new owner, a monster, picks up Elwis daily, eking out a number or two, and singing along. Naturally Elwis being the obedient servant.

Never thinking or even suspecting his fate. Then one drunken, drug high, party night monster decided to punish poor Elwis, to play and certainly not well, turned to Elwis to take out his anger and frustration. Naturally Elwis, being completely unsuspecting of what was coming, continued like always to make every effort to help his master make some semblance of music.

Not going well with all the bad ugly notes and sounds, the room heating up with drugs and his audience friends demanding something better. Now Mr. Monster begins to beat on our Elwis, fully demanding the impossible (The Stradivarius does not play it-self), the whole scenario most unfortunate for all. Drugs and drinks now peaking, Mr. M (M being for monster) loses control at the moment a string snaps. The pressure with all his frustrations imploded. "Bam!" Who's to suffer? Who's to pay? Elwis of course right there in the wrong place at the wrong time. Mr. M. decided everything gone wrong was to blame on Elwis. Now for the " branding "as the epitaph, almost as an inscription on a tomb. Mr. M with his trusty switchblade carved his initials in the front body of poor helpless Elwis. Being "EW." Now to be there for all to see forever and only the beginning of M's.". message" Within heightened rage. E is now thrown to the floor getting scratched and scuffed has his pegs broken and as the "coup de grace" M stomps down twice on E's neck, (upper part of the finger board) the break can be heard and painfully felt. This was almost E's demise. The party now being over and M feeling satisfied with finding his justice, took pleasure in discarding poor broken, scarred, pain ridden E down into the garbage ridden dumpster where he supposedly belonged. Next, a garbage man took a fancy to our broken friend and then home to his young son. He not being receptive to this now "basket case" passes E on to a buddy. E not at his best is discarded once again. Some-how now finding his way (scarred, broken, rippled and mangled) into the hands of all people, my grandson, Antonio and then me.

So as the later story will begin: Hiding in a closet waiting to come out, perhaps waiting for the next stomp or next dumpster. But no way .... the rest is history, our history. What a happy twist of fate for our Elwis....and for me, now together. The reader may now refer to narrative here, No, 51." Elwis And Me," for further happenings to our scarred friend, Elwis......Happy Reading......

Elwis And Me

Narrative No. 51
July 24th, 2021

The title for this individual narrative is " Elwis and Me" completely separate from all else. I thought this would be a logical beginning because it started in my mind with fictitious Narrative No.50. I'm so excited at this very moment. It's me and my guitar together alone. My guitar, Elwis of all names perhaps not so very appropriate for a guitar. But this is not just any G. Allow me to use G for guitar and E for my Elwis. This specific model of E happens to be an acoustical Yamaha F315A. A model that has been discontinued from Yamaha's manufacturing program.

All of this may be foreign, but meaningful to me. Everything having to do with E is meaningful. Let me try to say up front that I am beyond "taken" with E. Taken in many ways. The now playability, the playing sound. Sound be the basic heart and soul of a G.

This story begins when I first laid eyes on E. He was taken out of a closet and handed to me. My first reaction as always with any and all G's is to tune them. A very necessary and proper requirement. Gs cannot and should not ever be played out of tune. Reasons to be known to most everyone. The instrument cannot deliver a correct sound unless tuned. Correct by basic standards of music and the ear together. Be that as it may. He came out of the closet so badly out of tune. It was impossible for any adjustment. Unbeknown to me at that time was that E's neck was broken. Actually, and literally broken. Needless to say, that is beyond even an omen of death and certainly the death knell for any instrument particularly a guitar (poor E) we just kind of separated and E went back in his closet.

I honestly did not feel impressed at that first meeting. It was very apparent that he had been neglected and abused in a way that I had not ever seen before. Me not even realizing his broken neck. Also, to mention that some low life carved his initials, kinda cynically more as in jest than with any meaning. But all so appropriate for his distress it became. Instinctive that I sensed something different about this G realizing the damage and apparent major deficiencies. But back in the closet he went just the same. However, something impressed me.

A very short time later I inadvertently got involved in a very casual low-keyed plan to make a halfhearted effort to restore him. Low and behold the broken neck became apparent like it should have back when initially seen. That's when any fantasy of restoration was almost lost. However, with that mysterious something being, the thought became, to try.

Why not take the challenge for restoration, which truly appeared hopeless.?

So, the tedious work began, with Elwis as a good patient. The broken neck having to be the main focal point. Other defects being incidental and routine. Well, the neck was mended in a logical manner with glue splints and clamps. Knowing the excessive tensional stress imposed with 6 strings it was decided to have a lengthy curing period with the glue drying and clamps in place.

One week later all treatment was removed. And very apprehensive repair work continued, which basically consisted of cleaning excess glue off the neck wound. And then to install those killer strings, with new pegs, six to be exact. Knowing the threat of the neck bend failing and the stressful procedure, the anxiety was building, all in the next phase of tuning and that inevitable step of tightening the strings to tune, all in the necessity of arriving at playability.

Well, the mended neck did the job and sustained the string tension imposed. With the greatest attention and apprehension, the neck was under constant surveillance and concern. And low and behold it held and held well. Now Elwis is alive and well with a very likely bright future. With all the many guitars I've had and have Elwis remains special coupled with his mellow sound and remarkable playability. The knowing of his almost impossible resurrection makes him my favorite. Always conscious of his vulnerability to fail at the neck again. How foolish to attach such personal sentiment to just a wooden box with strings. But bear in mind with his "comeback" and the name Elwis certainly there is a special due here. And now waiting patiently to be exercised. (Played that is) let's get on with his new future and mine.

Right now, Elwis is performing well. I don't believe he knows he had his neck broken. He wants to play and sound normal. Maybe he is now. He was brought back. back from the grave, the grave of broken necks. It hurts just to say it. This is a guitar that wants to be played. Nice fingerboard, very nice" action." Great sound, maybe the best in the house. A masterful repair job was done and holding well. The future looks bright for this poor beat-up soul. I enjoy playing this guitar, better than my "Ibanez".

There is something special here. I'm trying to imagine this "box" as new and being happy. Now it's been resurrected, and maybe starting to realize it.

It's hard to identify what's so special here. Perhaps a lot of sympathy for a fallen comrade. Plays well, that's the phenomenon.

My friend Elwis will never be as good as new. But perhaps close. Will he sustain the tension of the six opposing strings for a day? For a week? for a month? for a year? We shall see. Time will tell.

I guess music became prevalent in my life. But it's my major form of recreation. I probably over-reacted with Elwis, but like I said repeatedly the sentiment was the whole spirit of the "resurrection," and then to end up with such a fine end result makes the entire scenario so extra special., and worthwhile. Let me work hard enough on my music studies so as to earn and deserve him.

I have overestimated Elwis' sound quality. I only heard what I wanted to hear. The poor guy is just hanging on for tune. But I love him just the same. I guess the neck rod adjustment potential would be "life" threatening. So be it, he's under my care now and trying hard!

This saga is sort of like the fallen. champion racehorse that broke its leg. Like a" Seabiscuit" story. Plenty of dramatical concern here, it's just the human-interest part that clings. Just a simple inexpensive guitar that met a bad fate. Certainly, a musical instrument cannot always be measured by dollar value ($). Here's a good case. This instrument may very well have a future. Broken neck not-withstanding. I'd like to own it and be a part of its future.

The cosmetic part of this restoration may not be so important. The playing and sound quality is the heart of the matter. It feels good to hold and to play and he responds accordingly. I still can't help feeling the apprehension and anxiety. I guess that's the challenge and thrill of it all. One day and one play at a time!

There is a lot of sentiment here. Having brought him back from the grave with a broken neck. I really wanted him!

Sat I had been on the phone part of the day. negotiating for Elwis with my grandson, and I finally won. All this scenario about an old beat - up, basket-case guitar, which may have come from the garbage. Nevertheless, I was determined to own him. So now the probable fate may be: My grandson gets two guitars from me, and I keep Elwis

The ultimate exchange finally was as follows: I did keep E as my own. I can't remember that good a feeling in a long while. However, this involvement over a musical instrument opened up the gate to unique sentimentality. Imagine all this over a basket case. I know my feelings centered over the fact of the improbability of restoration. Coupled with the strong sentiment for the guitar and the extent of such deliberate abuse. Along with the tender loving care for restoration, given by my son Anthony, all this made this miracle possible to happen. Elwis is here now, right beside me.

There is just so much you can expect here from my friend E. mended neck. New pegs, and strings carefully ever chosen: LaBella medium hard tension strings. Now very the discreet tender adjustment of (the fingerboard) neck rod, almost like new? Far be it. But together as a finished body E maintains a normal tuning mode. Naturally tuning is affected like all string instruments by temp.and humidity. Be that as it may. E is doing well. Certainly, the smooth playability as the characteristic of his smooth structure and design provides for the ease to play. Not sure of the actual extent of the aftereffects of the severity of a broken neck. Right now, I'm inclined to believe my Elwis is as good as he will get., And that's not so bad all things considered. There might be a fantasy hope to imagine betterment in sound later, with actually a slim possibility. But all in all, E is home safe and sound with me. This has been a fun experience which allows me to own and value a G in a special and different way now.

A much more intimate feeling beyond the normal expectancies, this kind of sentiment may possibly be applicable on to other types of musical instruments. However, my profoundness applies to strings. Why so strings? to justify, just basically the smooth tender effect on the ear. "Music soothes the Savage beast" most likely a string instrument.

Almost there. A final thought to consider the feel and comfort of holding my   guitar in a snug intimate mood. Now to go and exercise my fallen friend, and to truly enjoy the pleasure of his company. Such giant motivation for me to practice with so much gusto. Along with the potential to develop a better playing skill.

Perhaps I should have my neck broken and mended to be at an equal level with my friend E. (where's Anthony?) Imagine falling in love with a guitar? Silly? Elwis is sitting right next to me witnessing this whole writing. The thought that grabbed me here was the sentiment of saving a brutally abused instrument. I like the story. What do you think? Now for the right title. Maybe ....ELWIS And Me. I believe I now know what a "Grand Slam" feels like!

Two Separate Hearts Within One Body

Narrative No. 52
April 28, 2020

What if we did have two separate hearts working within one body? Working in unison with each other. Call one" left" and call the other "right". Just to allow for distinction.

Say the left was the working engine, providing for all the physical power required for all body functions and the right strictly for the emotional part, love, caring, concern, tenderness, , understanding, forgiveness, and a few other workings.

Stay with love, the biggest feature- It's warm, it's tender, and it's an important function. Naturally, the brain is in control and oversees both hearts completely with   positive distinction, The left is the workhorse, and the right is soft and angelic.

Love is a vital part of living, perhaps one of the strongest motivations. Love falls into many different categories, such as motherly love, family love, brotherly love, love for a child, and also as strong affection for one person to another. All perfectly normal emotions.

Now with the distinction of two separate hearts in one body, the wear and tear are consequently divided. The left is working physically harder, requiring more medical attention and physical care than the right. The right relieved of all heavy physical demands. It can function at an entirely different pace, which lends to its compatibility to be light-hearted, leisurely and dedicated to the important features of life, which is *love as a major purpose.* How comfortable and secure a feeling this is!

And just as necessary as food for fueling and as breathing for body functioning. But love is so special, as the cement that truly helps hold life together. Rich or poor is not necessarily a factor here, although it can become one. We always concern ourselves with how rewarding Love can be. Just a simple, casual thought of a loved one is fulfilling in itself. Then to be near; seeing, talking, touching, as the truest joy. The rapture in harmony and mutual relationship.

This thought or plan of two separate hearts in one body allows for the fullest advantage to have the right angelic heart free of bodily burden and focusing with all its pleasures on love, happiness, and all good things in life. This is an ideal fantasy, but fun just for us to imagine.

We all know that love, happiness, and caring have troubling moments and periods; some of tragedy, some of gloom, some of misunderstanding, and some of crisis. However, we say "Love Conquers All".

Big Thought- with-in the ideal lifestyle's existence, it certainly can be joyous, so we make the effort to find this real love thing and savor it. Just never to forget or take love and happiness for granted. It is to be worked as in a marriage. All are entitled to their fair share. Those born before this new concept of two hearts- perhaps extra transplants can be arranged! But where to find a donor?

First Date

Narrative No. 53
August 16, 2021

We met in the rain, and it could have been Spain, although not. But I certainly got that feeling when my heart went reeling, I started to speak, but then was too weak. Such beauty like never seen before. I jumped at the chance for this romance, and made my move to adore, now wanting more.

Did you know it was me at your front door? I would never come late for a first date. Her beauty was breathtaking, I tried not to be shaken. But I knew something wonderful just happened. What I have dreamt of forever and now is here before me. Can this be magic or love? Let's give it a shove

We shared a candle lit table; A glass of wine would be fine for our exchange. I was not able to believe my eyes, so mesmerized. And to know I'm near someone so dear. I felt a warm feeling when my heart went reeling. How foolish on a first date, to even expect to relate. It's so delightful to meet someone exciteful. We hardly know each other and yet we might discover something warm and special that we both have been looking for. Your eyes tell it all, that you know I'm to fall. This can't happen like this, without even a first kiss. Each time our eyes were to meet, the thought was to seek what was happening. To think this was real and to know how to feel such tender thoughts. A new kind of feeling warm with delight and never wanting to end this night.

Our date went well, it was easy to tell that she liked me. What wonders of wonder that we both came under the same kind of magic. For us not to have met would have been tragic. We make our next date and patiently wait. Again, I feel the same old reel.

This is what I want, someone to be near, someone so dear. Can she feel the same? Or is it just a game? She shows affection and my reaction is warm, just to hold her arm. A feeling so grand and when she takes my hand, I know it all, this is how you fall. Love cannot happen so fast, but perhaps the next best thing I ask. Our continuous dating proves our relationship.

Meet Mom and Dad and now I'm glad for what I found on some hallowed ground. She will serve me for life as my very wife. Children may come, just as to be. I can hardly wait to see. But then it all came to be, for her and for me, the blessing of true love, and my thanks to "above". Always with faith, life will reward, and both will

afford the best life can give for as long as we
both shall live.

The Barber Shop

Narrative No. 54
September 25, 2021

I love my Father, Antonino Michael Nisi, such a simple, loving, and uncomplicated man. Arriving here in America with his mother Rachel in 1907 at the age of 4. From Italia. His only wants were always to care and provide for his family. As well as anyone needing help. Settling in Chicago with two uncles and cousins. His Mother did not live long after. He was determined as a young man of 18 to find his long-lost father.

Through paisans the leads lead to Brooklyn, N.Y. His mother's sister, bedridden Aunt Louise took him in. Here with three cousins Raymond, Philip, and Mary all living together now in Queens, N. Y. However, finding his father had always been uppermost in his mind. Now his search led to a Barbershop in the Park Slope Section of Brooklyn.

The little tinkling bell on the door almost like an angel announced his presence after 18 years. The blue eyed giant over 6 foot tall, Michael Anthony Nisi was instinctively curious about this strange wanderer. Just another walk-in customer, most likely. After a casual greeting my father was then invited into the "throne", for just a routine everyday haircut. But not so routine, not so every day. I like to imagine it was a Tuesday. That being my pet day as uneventful. But not so this Tuesday.

Upon sitting down the curious eye contact by both, in the opposing barbershop mirror arrangement was electrifying for my father, He, knowing for sure who was now standing beside him after this almost lifetime absence, and now the search. But his father, not yet knowing his son, is sitting here beside him. The tenderness of this moment has taken over with such exciting inner emotions for my father alone. Speaking Italian in a rare Sicilian dialect started to arouse my grandfather

And in the casual conversation the mention by my father of some personal friends back in their hometown of Nicosia, Sicily really stirred my grandfather.

Perhaps coupled with a guilty conscience of having abandoned his wife and infant child and the fear of at long last being found. Gramps continuing to study this stranger with growing curiosity and growing trepidation, all through the mirrors, along with a growing fear. This giant is worried about being at long last discovered. All secure and confident in his hiding for so many years.

Now illegally remarried with five children all happy and safe in his Park Slope Brooklyn sanctuary. Maybe no longer? Then he suddenly seeing the marked resemblance a metamorphosis took place. The scissors echoing a sudden silence. Here was Antonino Michael Nisi sitting in his barber chair here in Brooklyn, far away from the land of their birth. His very son lost from so very long ago in a distant land, together at long last, in "The Barber Shop" ....

Ok- Monday Monday

Narrative No. 55
May 31, 2021

Ok- Monday as the inevitable start for my Memoirs that have been hiding. They tried to surface months ago, kind of suggested and encouraged by my daughter Diana, she very much interested in this book of mine, I presumptuously refer to it as "my writing." What I do haphazardly is record a fresh thought, a mood and or an impression like here now and try for. Memoirs: Which Mr. Webster tells me is a simple autobiography. That word frightens me.

I really would not intend to start to document my life at this time. Perhaps just briefly. First, let me pause to recognize May 31st as Memorial Day. A legal holiday in the U.S. in memory of the members of the armed forces killed in war. I've written a piece called "My Flag", (Narrative No. 1) which hit on some of my innermost feelings. I must pause right now and acknowledge this very special day. My military service was undoubtedly an important part of my life. It would not be at all possible here and now to sum it up. Let that be for another time, another essay, another book.

However, I must pause and try to express my sentiments right now. I can only hope that every American stops today to remember and somehow appreciate, although, appreciation is nowhere near enough. Just don't take this country for granted. Today not just being a great Monday off, People tend to their own pleasures. That's OK too, that's what heroes fought and died for, so Americans can have this freedom with all its "Liberties'".

Enjoy the holiday but let's never forget those brave heroes that make it all possible many that are not here to enjoy it too.

All brave Americans put their country first and foremost. The Flag as their faces, their voices, long may it wave. Now I'm on my way. I'll use age brackets as opposed to specific dates. Dates only when need be.

Start with the earliest recollection.as one of my favorite questions. As for mine, it was registration for my first day of school, me being 5 years old. Getting interesting? Stay with me, it's a long road. Somehow it was determined to start me in first grade, no kindergarten for me. First sign of brilliance. Perhaps first and last. But I did not feel brilliant. Still don't. However, I do enjoy my quips" Brilliance and Intellect can mix, they are compatible, just ask me ". Ok back to school. I Just got by no sign of brilliance.

Now graduating grammar school entering Jr. High school, still no brilliance around, where can it be? Good period, fun classmates. Good conscientious teachers.

Next off to high school. For some very unknown reason I chose an all-boy's school. A big mistake, I happen to like girls, and girls seem to like me. Now here I am in an all-boy's school for four years, no girls getting the chance to like me- Oh well," che-sera-sera." Graduated (academic diploma) in 1947. Slightly before my seventeenth birthday.

Started Night College, studying accounting, my mistake. Also working full time in lower Manhattan for an insurance firm, and of all things," mail boy" me with my academic diploma and now seventeen. Commuting on the Third Ave Elevated trains, open air cars in the warm season. Five cents fare each way, and the daily newspaper two cents, with first class postage three cents. Quart of milk at ten cents and a loaf of bread for eleven cents, gasoline for 17 cents per gallon.

Almost forgot to mention my very early vocational gig at about the age of eleven. A part time job in Abe's grocery just part time on Saturdays. One dollar for about ten hours plus tips (in the 193O'S) Tips which amounted mostly to stale cookies, after usually climbing 5 flights, not many elevator apartment houses in those days. Abe is determined to get his one-dollar Sat.'s worth. Had me in between deliveries, screening eggs to discard the blood shot ones. Very productive day, between the stale cookies and the bloodshot eggs.

I learned early that life would not be easy. No complaints because the bloodshot eggs were very impressive on my resume. I did however intentionally omit the stale cookies.

Back to the mailroom. Small, not much of a room but I did have my own phone, quite a distinction back then, at my start I could hardly wait to get home and tell my family and neighbors about my own phone.

Night school was trying, getting home late, tired, hungry, falling asleep in class. Accounting was boring and completely uninteresting, but it was a proud distinction then to be going to college. College to become a CPA. no less. But it reached a point of refusal. Dropped out after the first year.

Took several civil service exams for the U.S. postal service. Passed postal clerk, and

Letter carrier and ending up in the boondocks of Gun-hill Road in the Bronx, given the farmlands including all the dogs, who continued to chase me, and not quite catching up. But the snakes almost did.

Now for the highlight: I was appointed as a post-master, with my own post-office, "Feather-Bed Lane "substation in the Bronx quite a distinction at the age of 20. Then the Korean War broke out in June of 1950. Now being eligible and threatened by the military draft.

Decided to seek my fortune in California. Lived with my Aunt Rose and cousins. Four months of fun, but the draft was calling. And then on Monday April 29th, 1951, I was drafted (there's your" OK Monday, Monday"), inducted and sworn into the U. S. Army, Proudest day of my life. Started in the reception center at Ft. Devens Mass. K.P. stuffing ducks in the kitchen. Rained continuously, nonstop for one week. And me being in civilian clothes mostly, soaked in every oracle of my body. I assumed it would rain continuously for the next 21 months. The initial term of my draft tour, then extended to 24 months shortly thereafter.

The initial grueling experience for sudden conversion into a hard intimidating, demanding almost Impossible unbearable change from comfortable civilian life was somewhat traumatic.

But through it all I truly felt honored to have this opportunity to serve my beloved country. Even now 70 years later the thoughts still take my breath away.

I was dedicated to serve and do my duty. I had to do two cycles of boot camp training due to a death in my family. Later in Japan. Fortunate to advance to Section Chief of the communication center in Headquarters' Battery 63rd Field Artillery Battalion, 24th Infantry Division. Me as a low-ranking corporal in charge and leading sergeants. All attributable to the current administration's "freeze" on military funding. And me doing the job calling for sergeant first class as a corporal. Certainly not being much in favor, but doing my duty never-the- less, for $135 per month, In the rear reserves in war time. No false pretenses of heroics just serving my beloved country.

This being just a partial beginning as a Memoir, how to continue perhaps as a lengthy narrative? Already at 1233 words.

Joanne

Narrative No. 56
November 17, 2021

We met again in a Chicago blizzard November 1951.A few days before Thanksgiving. This story is true and only written now 70 years later, almost forgotten and lost in time.

Strange now for this recollection while it hardly crossed my mind in all these years. This is a curious moment of reminiscence. Joanne, a beautiful woman just about my age of 21 at the time. A very surprising meeting. Me a soldier in uniform, caught up in the intrigues of war.

My military destination was New Jersey to Seattle Washington by Troop Train. What a fascinating, enchanting experience cross country by train, with the unscheduled lay-over in Chicago, Because of a blizzard.

This recollection thrills me in many ways. Here in my twilight years that the memories of my military life now feel so poignant. Much different than the actual time living it and enduring the hardships and apprehensions, all as accepted. Heading with orders during the Korean war for the Far East.

Back to Chicago and Joanne during this November 1951, snowstorm. We, her and I were second cousins. Her Grand- Father, Uncle Vincenzo, was the brother to my father's mother Rachel., so we had the same great-grandparents, we as second cousins. Having previously met, many years before, so much younger on the Chicago family's visits with my family in New York, Cousins. Now reacquainting years later in this November blizzard, in snowy Chicago, near Thanksgiving. Everything happening was purely a quirk of fate and completely fascinating.

My first reaction knowing of this layover was to phone my father's uncle Vincenzo right from the train station. Those days of telephone directories made it easy to connect. Well, needless to say my Chicago family was ecstatic to hear from me and to know of my presence nearby at the train station. A short bus ride later there was our exciting reunion. Me along with my two G.I. buddies having this early Thanksgiving visit into a dinner of roast beef. With family, (Not quite prepared for turkey). What a warm feeling here and now to look back on such a meaningful happening. Lots of tender greetings and mutual exchange of family affection. So very special for all including my two unrelated army pals. We had a memorable snowball fight between three G.I.s, cousin Joanne and my father's aunt, (Sorry unable to remember her name) in this beautiful Winter Wonderland, Chicago.

There was a magic presence between Cousin Joanne and me. An affection beyond cousins. Close to infatuation all in the moment, partially I guess in the romance of war time and uniforms. The entire environment was love filled. And in such a surprise unplanned happenstance a strong bond with love was felt and made. Between Cousins,

We left and departed, off to war, after having had this wonderful visit and special celebration of reunion and "Thanksgiving." Resuming the train ride to Seattle, Washington, on to the Troopship," The Marine Adler." And 14 seasick days on the Pacific Bound for Japan, and who knows what? Remembering the spectacular dockside send off, in Seattle, For 3500 of us, with an army band playing: "So Long It's Been Good To Know You." Are we to survive and return home?

Me then to serve in the 63rd Field Artillery Battalion, 24th Infantry Division. Training continuously in Japan, in reserve, for the ongoing war in nearby Korea. The 24th was the first American military in Korea in June 1950, meeting with devastating losses attributable in part to extreme winter weather, Long before my joining them in Japan, in Dec 1951.

. Cousin Joanne, beautiful Joanne, home, far away in snowy Chicago. We corresponded intimately for my 18-month tour in Japan. But never to meet again since our Thanksgiving dinner 70 years ago in snowy Chicago. All gone, with this story as the only remaining trace. I wonder if she even remembered or thought of me or if she may even still be alive. Our brief encounter: all a beautiful tender memory for me now so very many years later with thoughts of, "What if...?"

I intentionally omitted A major factor, until now, in this brief romantic ...encounter. Cousin Joanne had been.... Newly Married to another, at that tender, precious time of our passing meeting and time of our intimate corresponding. Again, "What If...?"

Dear John

Narrative No. 57
September 20, 2021

You've heard about it, maybe even thought about how you would handle it and knew of a few real cases. But never did you expect to experience this thing up front and alive. Yes, it came. Came as a bolt of lightning and this time it didn't miss. Slam- Bam. Ouch.! Open that letter and weep. Meet "Dear John". Well, he's here and he found you. You were nice and cozy for about a year then it was your turn.

Her name was Bea, a Beautiful young lady. Lived With 4 older brothers, and sweet her being: their baby sister. Almost good for a Norman Rockwell Scene. We had been dating off and on as teenagers into maturity. Nothing steady just enjoyed each other's company.

Bea had a passion for dancing. In the late 40's the dance hall was a fun place to frequent, dance and make new friends. I am not much of a dancer but liked the action. We did care for each other and when I was drafted into the military it was the Korean War time. This whole thing of being yanked out of a cozy civilian life into "hell", distorts a relationship, inevitably. We were only dating casually but me going away and into harm's way did exaggerate feelings.

We were not going steady and never discussed any future relationship or plans, however during letter writing and with the element of loneliness and being apart, this remote romance grew. I felt a strong need for her which is normal under the circumstances. She missed me as well. So, our relationship did grow by mail.

Then it came...." Mr. Dear John." I didn't see it coming. I was serious minded about a relationship and thought about returning home and maybe marrying my Bea. Fun loving, pretty, nice to be with and with 4 hulking protective big brothers. Nice tapestry. Well after reading this "kiss-off." I didn't quite fully understand what happened when Bea dumped me. She never really had me to begin with.

She met this nice young fellow at a New Year's Eve party and was blown away and bye-bye Dom. I was shaken up and heartbroken only because of where I was, halfway around the world in harm's way and now without my Bea.

169

After the shock and feeling sorry for myself wore off. I accepted and adjusted to reality. Perhaps I would not have married her anyway. At that early stage of my life, I was not in a true mode of understanding meaningful love, maybe just a mild infatuation? Certainly, having longing, coupled with loneliness, given the circumstances.

But I did manage to survive. And rotated home after my 2-year tour of active duty. I was then to remain in the reserves for 5 years with the sum of 7 years' service.

Upon my return I was surprised to hear of Bea's regular visits to my folks. There she was waiting and happy and wanting to see me home. Her love for me had grown, notwithstanding her engagement for marriage to Mr. "Nice Guy". Here I now had this wonderful opportunity to take my now Bea swoops her up in my arms and fall in love. But that didn't happen. Not in this book anyway.

I did not love her and furthermore, far be it to be responsible for her engagement break-up. I chose to make that clear to my parent's "friend", Bea, whom I believe understood. Everything had been distorted mostly by me back then. And it was never meant to be. It saddened me somewhat, but the circumstances were very sensitive, and clear. Basically, it was my "call" and I walked. That" Dear John "did hurt just the same. But I did find the love of my life and moved on with absolutely no regrets. Make reference to my story no. 14 called ``Contemplation". Perhaps for regrets? Never! Perfect prologue for "Dear John" Also to read No. 58," At First Glance"., as a fictitious follow up to getting "dumped" ....such fun this writing game.......

At First Glance

Narrative No. 58
September 1, 2021

I composed this story, not just as a narrative but as something to share with real thoughts of Love. A fictitious imaginary happening. I hope the reading will be as pleasurable as the joy in writing it. Finding your own rainbow: "At First Glance". This may be "heavy" in a most loving way. Where it came from? I'll never know. The easy way is to say" THE HEART "

How does "it" start? What's the very first sign? Who would've thought she would ever be mine? Just a glance was enough to feel something warm, something new, but now to actually meet. She saw me too. Perhaps we both shared that same bit of excitement. Starting as a spark within. I don't know what just happened. But my heart knows. I try to get near for her to hear me say Hello. A smile says it all, just as it was meant to be. A few words were spoken, and we both knew what might be. A bit more of short conversation and we're both taken somehow. A wonderful feeling, perhaps the first sign of something special. A phone number is gotten here at the moment, without much thought of what just happened. Another sign of maybe attraction, to lead to where? Perhaps just a phone chat, no more than that. But just to hear her voice, stirs it all up again. That warm new feeling. A few more calls with some tender talk. And then the excitement to meet once more.

What will it be like? The same moving feeling? I know this is all different. Now a date, the first date. What does it all mean? Simply two people attracted, and now together. First meeting almost like a dream, no this is real. Here she is right beside me. And this feels so natural, to be so close and together.

The date finds its way with such a sure say. This is definitely the beginning of what I want, I want to be with her. The phone calls are good but together is better. I hold her hand and can feel the sign of excitement. A happiness of a new and special kind. I found the girl of my dreams. Now wondering how she might feel about me.

Love can be at first sight, perhaps that can then become a thing to grow. I am taken and wanting to be together at every chance. It is physical. I can feel the excitement of being together. And when she's near it's the best kind of feeling. When we're apart there's that empty spot in my heart. Infatuation may be possible and even likely. A quick reaction to the attraction. But that soon becomes defined, when she is always on my mind, as we both anxiously await each next date. I'm Had, I can't be without her, which makes for a good thing for both to have found each other. She has all the same feelings as I.

Such could happen with no uncertainty here. This is what love can be and now is, you felt it's presence, The magic of it all. A casual chance meeting to become my very life, and now my very wife. Together as one. The always nearness, what we both want.

No greater being as this lifetime commitment: together thru sickness and in health. Now for the part of "having it all"; Children, what closer bond than that of Family?

I live with all this love and thrill with it all, now with my partner for life. Working together and living the life that dreams are made of. Through hard times and wonderfully good times shared with all, together as one and as family. Always there for each other for all times, and to

174

continuously grow together with the love that started it all. And now to pass it on the way we received our blessings. Always to remember the miracle of that first enchanted meeting. Beauty was present, but not even spoken. It stems from your heart and is seen to be true.

How beautiful this entire romance is, all as seen through loving eyes and will always stay that way. This love has its own beauty that keeps the heart beating, all which grows stronger as the years flee by.

All the blessings. The blessings to have her as my wife and as the Mother of our children. It's all so natural. Love has no need for an engine. The power is there always with all the grace as strong and even stronger than day one. This miracle of love is the fuel through the years, making all tears as happy ones. No matter what, joy is from the togetherness of having and sharing it all. Bringing the Family together as one and as strong as ever.

The roots of life always to share with my wife. Forever and perhaps into the next life, even stronger. Our paths did cross and that first casual glance became a lifetime romance. All......." At First Glance" ....